FLYING SCOT

FLYING SCOT

An Airman's Story

Air Commodore Alastair Mackie

Pen & Sword
AVIATION

First published in Great Britain in 2012 by
PEN & SWORD AVIATION
An imprint of
Pen & Sword Books Ltd
47 Church Street
Barnsley
South Yorkshire
S70 2AS

ISBN 978-1-84884-756-9

Typeset by Concept, Huddersfield, West Yorkshire
Printed and bound in England by
CPI Group (UK) Ltd, Croydon, CRO 4YY

Pen & Sword Books Ltd incorporates the Imprints of Pen & Sword Aviation, Pen & Sword Family History, Pen & Sword Maritime, Pen & Sword Military, Pen & Sword Discovery, Wharncliffe Local History, Wharncliffe True Crime, Wharncliffe Transport, Pen & Sword Select, Pen & Sword Military Classics, Leo Cooper, The Praetorian Press, Remember When, Seaforth Publishing and Frontline Publishing

For a complete list of Pen & Sword titles please contact
PEN & SWORD BOOKS LIMITED
47 Church Street, Barnsley, South Yorkshire, S70 2AS, England
E-mail: enquiries@pen-and-sword.co.uk
Website: www.pen-and-sword.co.uk

To Rachel,
who shared my joys and sorrows,
triumphs and disasters
for more than sixty-seven years.

Contents

Chapter 1

Something in the Air

In the sleepy Worcestershire town of Malvern in the twenties we hardly ever saw actual aeroplanes, although books and pictures of them had fascinated me since early childhood. On one memorable day, however, there arrived a flying circus – not Monty Python's, but a real one.

It was owned and operated by Sir Alan Cobham, who had been a First World War pilot. He had a miscellany of elderly aircraft, including an Avro biplane in which he offered punters short flights – hops, more like – for payment. I was crushed by my father's refusal of my plea to be taken aloft. This was not, I think, because of the cost, but he was rather thinking of the danger.

The offering of these flights was known as 'barnstorming'. Fast forward to my own flying days and I, like most pilots, had the job of giving cadets and other would-be airmen such flights so they could gain 'air experience'. On one occasion, a boy from Eton College Air Training Corps thanked me for his flight and offered a tip. *Noblesse oblige*, or what?

There were no such offerings from ATC cadets from my own school, Charterhouse. Like other public schools, we were visited by liaison officers recruiting for the three services. At the time of one such visit, in July 1940, I was semi-idle, having passed the exams that qualified me to go to Christ's College Cambridge to train as a doctor.

One evening, I went to an excellent lecture by a naval officer that propelled me into wanting to take part in a war that I feared would end before I could become involved. I thought of the Army, but was put off by the *sotto voce* assurance that those of us who joined up in the ranks of the local regiment, the 60th (Royal Surrey) Rifles, and behaved ourselves, would within six months be commissioned as officers. This, I felt, flouted my principle of paddling my own canoe. The Navy, in a sense, might have requited that. But life as a seaman seemed to consist of very long stretches of gazing at oceans and only rare opportunities for the sort of derring-do I had in mind.

That left the RAF. I consulted my father about deferring the medical training for which I had been promised; there would be a place for me at Cambridge after the war. Patriotically, he encouraged me to join.

During my final term at Charterhouse I had to go to a centre in Reading for medical testing, which turned out to be very thorough. On the way back from Reading I passed through Waterloo Station, where, to my surprise and delight, I saw King George VI – in field marshal uniform and in a Rolls-Royce – drive through the main entrance.

I soon heard that I had passed the medical test, which wasn't a surprise to me as I had always done my best to keep fit. Hopeless at football and a source of despair at cricket, I had resorted to tennis, squash and swimming, and these were soon to become sources of personal delight and points scoring from the RAF. There were squash courts at most airfields, and I used them enthusiastically until I reached the recommended age limit of forty.

Following my medical test a telegram summoned me to report to the RAF Records Office in Gloucester. This was a daunting surprise because I had hoped I would go to a training unit rather than a mere repository for personal particulars. Thankfully, it was simply part of the bureaucracy. I thought of Shakespeare's dictum:

There's a divinity that shapes our ends,
Rough-hew them how we will ...

I was relieved when a posting to Cardington for initial training arrived. Even that seemed odd, because Cardington was well known as the centre for the RAF balloons that became integral to air defence. I was soon to discover that it also housed a reception centre for processing recruits. This comprised swearing them in, giving them the traditional King's shilling and equipping them with their much-prized uniform.

Going through the system took all day and meant an overnight stay in a barrack block. My bed was one of thirty; occupants of the other twenty-nine insisted on keeping their underwear on and the windows shut on a warm August evening. The smell was awful.

Towards the end of a second day of processing it emerged that we were expected to stay another night, up with which (in the manner of Churchill) I would not put. I explained to the corporal in charge that I had friends nearby who I could stay with. He was surprised and told me that the railway warrants we were to be issued with had not yet been signed and that the flight lieutenant whose job it was to sign them had gone off duty. When I volunteered to go without one he let me go.

My destination was a large house at Ickwell, where a Mr and Mrs Hayward Wells would, I knew, be glad to put me up for the night: no smells, no underwear making do for pyjamas, and every comfort. Mary Wells was a lifelong friend of my mother's and Hayward part-owned the brewing firm of Wells and Winch, which was eventually to be taken over by one of the big breweries – Greene King – in 1961. The Wells welcomed young officers as guests during the war, me included.

Thus began the humble first phase of my RAF career, which was known as deferred service but turned out to be a boring wait in the queue for full-time training.

Chapter 2

The Wide Blue Yonder

Back home, after what seemed an intolerable wait, I was thankful to get what I came to know as a summons – to Torquay, where there was an initial training wing (ITW) for new recruits. There, along with a batch of other would-be aircrew, I learnt such elemental skills as marching, saluting, good turnout and, perhaps most importantly, discipline. I was placed in a squad where an outwardly severe sergeant who was inwardly wise and tolerant did his job admirably, although his assistant, a corporal, was afflicted with an urgency complex that was revealed by his custom of shouting, 'c'monurryup.'

We were billeted in requisitioned hotels and slept three or more to a room. For no obvious reasons, each hotel had to be guarded by a sentry detailed on a roster to stand by the front doors during daylight hours – a highly unpopular job. One lucky member of the squad was agreeably surprised when an elderly woman passer-by remarked that he looked tired and gave him a pound – a considerable sum at the time. Needless to say, all the other squad members, me included, did our best to look tired, to no avail.

Together, the sergeant and his assistant taught us the elementary skills, using the adjoining tarmacked area for marching and drill. One day during square-bashing, a youth had the temerity to try and cycle across the tarmac. The sergeant showed his alacrity and strength by grabbing the boy and the bike and literally stopping them in their tracks. Otherwise, the six-week training period was well spent and, in its way, enjoyable, not least because of the kindness of the management of the Imperial Hotel.

In retrospect, my time in Torquay did me a power of good. I was physically fit and, with due diffidence, well disciplined and self-respecting. After home leave I was posted to Sywell, one of a highly regarded network of elementary flying schools dating back to before the Second World War and operated by Marshalls of Cambridge – a commercial flying school. The instructors were civilians commissioned into the RAF and given ranks that corresponded with their status. I was allotted flying officer equivalent David Bamford, who proved to be as pleasant personally as he was skilled professionally. As a further bit of luck, Sywell was equipped with DH 82 Tiger Moths, acknowledged as one of the best elementary training aircraft.

I took to it like a fish to water, being, as I was to discover years later when I was an instructor myself, one of a very small minority of so-called natural pilots. This delighted me and made David Bamford's job all the easier. We followed the standard sequence of exercises, culminating in the aerobatics that I enjoyed most. Compared with him, I was timorous and hesitant about such difficult manoeuvres as looping, stall-turning (climbing steeply, doing the turn, and letting the aircraft fall out of the sky down to the safe height of 3,000 feet). I was a mere tyro compared with Bamford, who was expert at the tricky business of inverted flight. Like almost all pilots he eventually overdid it: his sad demise happened because he fell into a common trap – overconfidence. Sharing with him, as I did, a propensity for showing off, I might well have fallen into the same trap myself.

My next posting – the RAF College Cranwell – was where serious flying training meant submitting to severe discipline. Cadets who strayed from the straight and narrow were thrown out, without any second chance. There was very little to be overconfident about because the trainer was the twin-engined Airspeed Oxford. Docile apart from a habit of darting off, like errant cadets, from the straight and narrow, it offered a useful lead-in to would-be bomber pilots.

Cranwell, apart from being an AFTS (Advanced Flying Training School, to signify progression from EFTS – Elementary Flying

Training School), had kept the excellent pre-war facilities in a truncated form. The staff did all they could to uphold pre-war standards. The college had a slogan: '*Superna Petimus*,' roughly meaning 'strive for the very best.' This was a shade more positive, perhaps, than the slightly masochistic '*per ardua ad astra*' (through adversity to the stars) conferred on the RAF as a whole.

We were treated like flight cadets. Like our forbears, we were expected to live up to the standards implicit in the title 'Flight Cadet' and their arrogantly titled 'Gentleman Cadet' peacetime Sandhurst equivalents. That sobriquet wasn't always justified. My half-brother, William Collingwood, for example, celebrated his passing-out parade with a drunken escapade of sinking the band as it played for the farewell ball from a floating stand on the ornamental lake. Flight cadets earned a parody of Chaucer that appeared in a 1920s' issue of the *College Journal*, preserved in Hilary St George Saunders' excellent history of British air power 1911–1939, *Per Ardua* (1945):

> *His buttons on parayde were bryte,*
> *His puttyes always laced were y-tight*
> *And never fowle or muddie were his hoon*
> *He always did his preparacioun.*

Apart from the very few promoted from the ranks, almost all flight cadets were ex-public school boys. Until the war, flight cadets, on graduation, took up the lordly, leisurely existence, as it was described, of squadron service in peacetime.

Spared puttees (hot and uncomfortable leg bandages, which I had worn in the Officers' Training Corps), we did our best to keep standards up. We lived in comfort in the old college, two to a single room. My roommate was Reg Langley. Older than me and a Lancashire lad, he was unaffected and a source of good advice, not least about cars. We were friends for all too short a period because he was to die in action in little more than a year.

Just as I landed and pulled up after my first solo in an Oxford I saw a small aircraft being towed from its hangar, some distance from the control tower and other hangars. Astonishingly, it had no propeller. It was the original jet-propelled aircraft fitted with Air Commodore Whittle's prototype jet engine, invented in the late 1930s while he was still a flight cadet. The engine prompted none too serious a distinction: pistons were said to depend on fans on the front and jets sucked themselves along.

After circuits came cross-country flying, putting into practice the elementary navigation and map reading learnt in the ground school. It provided a frightening break in my self-satisfied progression towards getting my wings. My earnest but unremarkable flying partner, Leading Aircraftsman Bob Jackson, and I did the required number of navigation exercises, one of which was following a triangular route south of Cranwell. After doing the sums and plotting the course we set off on a cloudy April day, flying as briefed at 2,000 feet. The cloud base soon lowered and we continued on instruments. I was driving and Bob was navigating with the map on his knee. We descended to 1,500 and then to 1,000 feet and were still in cloud.

Then it happened.

As we were debating whether to turn for home, part of a huge vertical steel girder flashed into view, inches from the starboard wingtip. We both realized that it could only be one of a clutch of 1,300ft wireless masts near Rugby. At any second we could collide with one of the others. A few interminable seconds later it was apparent that we had passed through the terrifying obstacle. Just as I was asking what we should do next, Bob vomited. The clouds soon lifted and knowing from our frightful encounter where we were, we flew back to Cranwell and decided to say nothing. Only now do I reveal the truth.

We soon began night flying at Cranwell's satellite airfield, Barkston Heath. We found it none too difficult because of an overarching fear. LAC Patrick finished his dual instruction and was sent off to do the canonical single circuit and landing. Having completed it, he taxied into the changing-over area, where the ground crew noticed with alarm that the aircraft was spattered with bullet holes. It transpired that a German intruder aircraft, then not an unusual visitor to eastern England, had followed Patrick round his circuit and fired on him. So intent had he been with the task in hand that he had had no idea of what was happening. Thereafter we all practised not just night circuits but also doing them with a swivelling head.

By now we were experienced enough for the dawn chore of ferrying the aircraft back to Cranwell, longing for food and sleep. At that time in the morning it was still cold and nothing would have persuaded us to take off our overcoats. Being trusted with this task and given a gruelling final handling test signified we were aviators competent enough to be given wings – yet another priceless boost to my self-esteem.

It soon became clear that the commerce of the day recognized a chance to cash in on the glamour attributed to wings by the admass. A particularly ghastly instance came from the jewellery industry:

> *Cheers, cheers, you've got your wings,*
> *Now you can buy me some Bravington rings.*

Chapter 3

Ready for Take-Off

Emerging from my airman's hairy chrysalis I reflected on how well the RAF had cared for me and my friends. We were made to keep fit, clean and smart. We had to keep reasonable hours. The perception that airmen were encouraged to drink too much had proved false. The medical officer had given us the sort of fatherly talk that few real fathers could have steeled themselves to deliver, such as the purpose and technique relating to condoms.

Our morale was sky-high and we chafed to get into action. Years later, as a station commander, I was proud to witness a similar metamorphosis that turned conscript youths from the pond life of urban street corners into fit, self-respecting contributors to the RAF and the wider community. Four of the best were kept well drilled and smart, ready for the station's quota for escorts at Winston Churchill's funeral.

Briefly at home, I walked the Malvern Hills and no doubt bored everybody by recounting my unremarkable doings. I was thrilled by the not unexpected news that I would be commissioned as an acting pilot officer on probation on 11 May 1941. On the 10th I went to London to be measured for my uniform at Burberry's, Cranwell's tailor of choice. I also opened an account at Lloyds Bank in Pall Mall, in which all officers whose names began with the letters L-Z had their pay deposited. For me it amounted to 14s 6d per day plus £30 for uniform. The latter took so long to arrive that I feared there had been a mistake and I was really only a sergeant.

I stayed the night at what was then the Royal Empire Society, in Northumberland Avenue. Such was the noise of an air raid that, unable to sleep, I made my way onto the roof. What I saw was surreal. All around were fires, the biggest stretching for miles eastward. (Years later, when I became Under-Treasurer of the Middle Temple, I discovered that, along with the Inner Temple, it had been partly destroyed at that time.) I had felt more angry than frightened. I was glad that my twin-engined training, almost certain to lead to a bomber posting, would offer a chance to hit back.

The chance soon came. With Reg Langley and other friends I was sent to the RAF station at Harwell, near Oxford, for operational training on Wellington bombers. That was another stroke of luck. Following the customary principle of safety in numbers, the Air Ministry had developed three different types. The Whitley was slow and cumbersome. The Hampden was faster but could only carry a small bomb load and, because it had no second pilot, was regarded as relatively dangerous. The Wellington, however, was larger and faster, carried two pilots and had had a criss-cross Duralumin skeleton, like a waste paper basket and known as 'geodetic', which gave it great strength.

The Bristol Pegasus engines fitted to the early version of the Wellington were barely powerful enough, but later ones had Rolls-Royce Merlins and then Pratt & Whitney Twin Wasps, both of which gave it an excellent performance. Nicknamed 'the Wimpy' after the cartoon character J. Wellington Wimpy, it became the staple of the medium force, more than 11,000 having been built. It was to have been replaced by the more powerful Vickers Warwick but better successors were the new trio of four-engined aircraft. Warwicks, however, were useful for transport and air/sea rescue.

Compared to Oxfords, the Wellington was lumbering and heavy to fly. In particular, the long sequences of rods and linkages between the throttle controls and the engines imposed an irritating delay, much like the soggy response of a pipe organ compared with that of a piano. Juggling with the throttles to make the small adjustments needed for a decent approach was formidably difficult at first, not much eased by the instructors, who were untrained as such, being bomber pilots who had completed a tour of operations, mostly over Germany. The good ones had useful tips to impart. Others were 'line shooters', giving exaggerated and ill-advised accounts of their adventures.

Many years later, I paid a nostalgic visit to the aircraft museum at Brooklands, which lacked a Warwick but not a Wellington. Showing off, as usual, I told a family viewing the Wimpy that I had flown it during the Second World War. They looked incredulous and insisted on photographing what they obviously saw as two museum exhibits.

Ready for long cross-country flights, the student pilots were paired off and crewed with a navigator, a wireless operator and rear gunner. Our newly trained navigators often got lost, and the instructors were seldom more useful than the rest of the crew. Help usually came from wireless bearings to augment and rectify the dead reckoning, the term of art for basic navigational computation. Help also came from the pilot's map reading and the pinpoints provided from his rear view by the gunner. Our most spectacular trip, in preparation for the forthcoming ferry flight to the Middle East, took us northwards into the eastern Atlantic to Rockall, a solitary rock that took skill and luck to find. Then came combat training, with practice bombs and air firing from the Boulton Paul turret, a mechanical marvel from which the gunner could swivel, raise and lower his four Browning machine guns. We got fewer practice flights than we would have liked.

For the forthcoming ferry trip I was teamed with Pilot Officer John Tolson, formerly a junior in the Asiatic Petroleum Company, a predecessor of Shell. In a rare burst of modesty, I have to admit that he was a better pilot than I; but we shared the flying equally, taking captaincy in turns. He was a charming, effervescent man, full of energy and humour. The other members of the crew were the navigator, Sergeant Bolton, wonderfully precise with his charts, no doubt because he had been a trainee town planner, Sergeant Jimmy Worden, formerly an office boy at the *Daily Mirror*, streetwise and cocky, and Louie Warren, much older and a former layer of granite floors in Belfast. He liked the job of rear gunner, being, as he explained, indifferent to where he was going but keen to see where he had been. Before trips he habitually peed on the under-carriage for luck – a superstitious practice later banned because urine damaged the metal.

Harwell was one of the network of RAF stations built in the 1930s as part of the re-armament that started after the dream of a peaceful post-war world had faded. They were widely separated at different heights above sea level to mitigate the problems of cloud and fog and to effect dispersal. The station had to accommodate many more people than it had been designed to take, but it was comfortable and in beautiful rural surroundings, not far from my home in Malvern.

I had used savings accumulated during my early years to buy an Austin Seven, its foibles seen to by Reg Langley. It was an attraction for the ample sufficiency of WAAFs.

I spent a final few days in Malvern; a gloomy period that included mourning my West Highland terrier Tinker (originally named Tinker-bell when she was given to my sister and, unkindly by my father, Stinker, and later, Stencher). On my last day's leave I drove my Austin Seven back to Harwell, parking it in the drive of a house nearby. That was a facility kindly provided by the owner, a doctor friend of my father's, who was happy to keep it there until my mother could collect it. He asked me in and listened to my story to date, being visibly moved and blushingly appreciative. He was sure, I sensed, that I was going to be killed. The insight led me to write a letter to my parents to be posted in the event of my death, which was happily never to be sent:

> In my nineteen years I could not have had a happier life ... I have thought of you and home as a steady, different world to which I aimed to return and looked upon as a support; having that behind me, my job has been easy. Think of all that I've had in my life, not what I've missed. My death was probably in

the thick of a raid or in the instantaneous finality of a flying accident – painless and probably happy.

Wilfred Owen, it isn't. But not too bad, perhaps, for a teenager. Thus ended my youth.

Chapter 4

Go East Young Man

At last, on 29 August 1941, we left Hampstead Norris, the satellite airfield for Harwell, Gibraltar-bound. At full power, in which state the Pegasus engines would have gasped and clattered, the Merlins purred, and we left the runway like a scalded cat.

The easy bit was finding Bishop's Rock lighthouse and turning for Cape Finisterre at the north-west tip of Spain. Getting there was the difficult bit because it meant passing the French port of Brest and evading the attentions of the German fighters based there by getting under the radar. The standard way of flying as low as possible was to wait for the long trailing aerial behind us to earth (or sea, rather) itself and put the radio out of action. When that happened, John Tolson and I enjoyed more low-flying practice in an hour than we had done in weeks of training. Remembering that the 29th was my father's 63rd birthday, I reflected that it would be as well not to get killed, and so took particular care as I savoured the intoxicating thrill of going faster and lower than ever before.

No fighters appeared and we rose to a sedate height, Bolton's skill taking us to Cape Finisterre and thence to Cape St Vincent, the south-western extremity of Iberia. We had been warned of Gibraltar's Levanter cloud, which sometimes enveloped the Rock for days, as well as the capricious winds; neither materialized. We rounded the Rock at Europa Point and landed safely on Gibraltar's very short runway.

17

On the way to Malta one of Bolton's miscalculations took us too close to the Italian islet of Pantellaria (virtually unknown in the West until it was recently used as a base for the swatting of Colonel Gaddafi), putting us at risk of interception from the mainland. That possibility became a certainty when we encountered the enemy, fascinated to have finally got to the war. This took the form of an ancient flying boat (very similar, for the experts, to the contemporary Saunders Roe London of the RAF). Louie Warren was desperate to get his guns on it but the right course was not to dally by turning, but to make for Malta as quickly as possible, hoping that the fighters they would summon from Italy would not jump us. Happily, they didn't appear.

Arriving in Egypt and hoping for more action, our hopes were dashed. We were dumped into a foetid transit camp called the Middle East Pool to await posting to a squadron. Every new arrival got diarrhoea, in some cases with vomiting. The only relief in this squalid sojourn came from listening to the BBC Overseas Service, whose nightly news bulletin ended with comments from Alan Murray, a family friend living in Malvern, near the broadcasting station. He was no Alastair Cooke, nor, another giant of those days, Raymond Graham Swing. But I found him an enjoyable link with home.

After what seemed an interminable wait, we were allotted to 108 Squadron, just re-formed and reviving a famous number, based at Fayid, where there was a Lysander, well known for clandestine spy-dropping in France but used at Fayid as a runabout. The commander was Con Wells, a buccaneer of the Norfolk squirearchy with a sense of humour that did not detract from his authority. He proved to be a born leader and soon developed the air and ground crews into an efficient unit, ready, willing and able for raids. When, as happened from time to time, he had something to complain about to the staff at Group (205) Headquarters, he would jump into the Lysander and tell the staff, not too politely, what he thought of them.

One of the flight commanders was a senior, very experienced pilot who had taken part in the recent evacuation of our land and air forces from Greece during that tragic operation. As captain of a Sunderland flying boat, which he had retrieved from under the advancing Germans' noses, he had as his sole passenger a female British refugee. During the flight back to Egypt he had paid a courtesy call to ensure that all was well with her. Together they created a unique circumstance for the award of a Distinguished Flying Cross, fully complying with the requirement that it should be 'in action'.

Spare time at Fayid was plentiful and finding ways to use it was a problem. One way of relieving it was exploring the local Arab villages. Dressed in long robes known variously as *dhotis* and *galabeas*, the men wore white skullcaps and the women headscarves. They lived in primitive huts and cultivated land made fertile by the periodic flooding of the Nile. They looked well fed, never begged and were welcoming, and especially enjoyed having their photographs taken.

Fayid was a half-built station still peopled with Arab workmen none too fastidious about where they performed their bodily functions. At the time there were accusations, probably justified, that German bombers jettisoned their loads rather than drop them on their designated targets, which was labelled 'indiscriminate bombing'. The medical officer at Fayid described the Arabian incontinence as 'indiscriminate shitting'.

The messes were in half-completed barrack huts and everybody lived in huts appropriate to their ranks. Apparently abandoned on the airfield was an old relic of an aeroplane, a Fairey Gordon. It was a biplane light bomber of the 1930s, delightful to handle and the first in the RAF to be fitted with wing flaps to reduce the landing speed and provide an easier landing attitude. Sadly, some idiot crashed it, damaging it beyond repair.

Longer spells of time off, and free transport, enabled us to pay a weekly visit to Ismailia, an elegant town in the Delta with a French club, of which officers were made honorary members. Our horrible diet in the mess made the club's cuisine all the more of a delight.

The route back to Fayid ran along the Treaty Road connecting Cairo and Suez, built as part of the Anglo-Egyptian agreement for the stationing of British troops in Egypt. A landmark was the checkpoint halfway along the road used to stop traffic when it was militarily necessary. One day during a ban the sentries stopped a large car carrying a single, very fat passenger. On being told to turn back, he protested that he was Farouk, King of Egypt. The sentry replied that he was Winston Churchill and repeated the order with a threat to shoot if it were not obeyed. The incident was said to account for the fact that British forces in Egypt received no thanks, let alone the medal that would have been appropriate.

Our first venture as a crew was to fly up and down over Cairo at night to give target practice to Egyptian anti-aircraft artillery. Just before we began the necessary straight and level runs at sitting-duck height, an Egyptian voice on the common control frequency was heard to ask whether live or blank ammunition was to be used. We sheered off until a British controller assured us that the gunners now knew it was to be the latter.

It was a relief to start proper operations, not least because, ever since I decided to join up, it looked like the war might end before I could get to it. Preparations for a raid began with flight planning and main briefing. Then came the oversight of the bombing-up of our aircraft and often the stowage of bundles of multilingual tract-like leaflets intended to subvert the opposition and any pro-enemy Senussi tribesmen rumoured to be in the habit of cutting off genitals. To encourage them to release any of us that they took prisoner we also carried multilingual papers offering a reward for letting us go. After loading came final preparation for our departure from the comfortable base to one or other of the advanced landing strips that would put us within range of our target. Fully loaded and fuelled, our well-worn Wellingtons seemed to stagger into the air in the blinding heat of the afternoon.

The landing strips had few facilities other than fuel tankers, a handful of ground crew, a workshop and rest tents. The one advantage was the proximity of the strips to the sea. The ground, and occasionally aircrews enjoying a temporary respite, took full advantage. We were glad when our turn came. It made a welcome change from climbing into the night sky in our elderly aircraft for attacks on Italian targets in Cyrenaica. They were chosen to support the Eighth Army as it continued the series of advances and retirements that had started in 1940–41. The opposition consisted of flak and fighters; the latter, Italian at first, but later, their more efficient German counterparts.

The target assigned to us for our first raid was Tobruk. We were surprised and delighted to get a direct hit on a ship in the harbour estimated to be a 5,000-tonner, happily confirmed by photo reconnaissance and reported, to my parents' delight, in their local paper – the *Malvern Gazette*. Back at base, I was saddened to learn of the loss of two friends. One was my former captain and co-pilot John Tolson, who was killed over Benghazi. The other was my Cranwell roommate, Reg Langley, who failed to return from a torpedo attack on shipping in the port of Piraeus, near Athens. To my shame I lacked the moral courage to tell his wife Eileen of the near-certainty that he would have been killed. It later transpired that he probably died flying his crippled aircraft into an enemy ship. Eileen remained a friend; she became godmother to my eldest son and we corresponded for many years until she died.

We were unlucky ourselves when, on a flight to an advanced landing strip fully loaded and fuelled, an engine failed. That was a considerable emergency. The Wellington could barely maintain height because the propeller on the failed engine would not feather. Having practised the emergency many times, but, acutely aware that there could be no second chance, I landed with the same mixture of skill and luck that had favoured us at Tobruk.

There was soon great excitement at the news that our ancient Wimpys were to be replaced with four-engined American B-24 bombers delivered directly from the Consolidated Aircraft factory in the USA. They were laps of luxury in comparison with the cold and cumbersome Wimpys. Some of them had messages from Consolidated workers, some rather blush-making, hidden in a hollow fitment that secured the control columns.

Instead of settling down to our change of type, however, the 'powers that were' decided that we were to return to Britain by troopship. We were airlifted in a Dakota across Africa to Takoradi, via Khartoum, El Fasher and Geneina. Known as the Takoradi Run, it was the ferry route for aircraft, usually fighters, shipped to Lagos and flown to the Middle East with an escort for guidance. There were, alas, many casualties among the inexperienced ferry pilots.

We thought our stay would be brief but it was not to be. We were stuck there for six weeks, towards the end of which I developed malaria. I was admitted to the civilian hospital in Lagos. As I was getting better I was horrified to see from the ward that the troopship *Georgic*, formerly a luxurious cruise ship, which was to take me back to the UK, had docked. Though still very weak, I discharged myself and staggered the short distance between the hospital and the dock. Once on-board I soon recovered.

The *Georgic* was fast enough to sail unescorted and still luxurious. All went boringly well until the captain, joining us in the bar, explained that the vibration we were experiencing was due to the full speed ahead needed to outpace a pursuing German submarine. Happily, it worked and we docked at Gourock on the Clyde.

Chapter 5

Chasing the Dawn

My disembarkation leave gave me welcome respite at home. The reason for returning to the UK, however, was that it had been decreed that I do a Liberator conversion course, despite having been amply converted in Egypt. This took place at a god-forsaken base in Yorkshire.

Complying with another edict from on high we collected a Liberator, newly arrived from San Diego, at the transatlantic terminal at Prestwick. The rigours of an overnight train journey were mitigated by sharing a first class compartment with two young ladies whose enthusiastic companionship most agreeably, but exhaustingly, exceeded expectations. We flew a newly arrived Liberator back to Lyneham (which had been the main RAF overseas arrival and departure point until it closed in 1912), and thence, a few days later, back to the Middle East. This time the destination was a base in Palestine, reached in two hops – a welcome change from the wearisome three that the Wellington delivery in 1941 had needed.

The first raid I did was a daylight attack on a harbour in Crete. It was an interesting change, being the first since heavy losses had ended Blenheim daylight raids in 1940. The next task was a wearisome series of shuttle flights delivering naval torpedoes to Malta, still under siege, from both Gibraltar and Egypt. There followed a raid on the Corinth Canal in Greece, a year to the day after I had bombed it in a Wellington. On both occasions we had the benefit of special helpers. One was a flight lieutenant with contacts in Greece, who helped at the briefing on both occasions with the welcome news that there were ships in the canal that would be trapped if we managed to block it at both ends. The 'both ends' bit reminded me of the mythical, self-confessed rogue's confession:

> *I burn the candle at both ends,*
> *It will not last the night,*
> *But, oh my foes and oh my friends,*
> *It gives a lovely light.*

This is just what the Greek underground patriots who lit fires on the high ground on both sides of the canal did. Long after the Second World War ended I went back to Corinth as part of my work for CND and marvelled at the skill, or more probably luck, that had enabled us to succeed.

We also did a series of other raids, mostly alternating between Benghazi and Tobruk. Although we suffered flak damage, the losses were unexpectedly low. A sad exception was the shooting down of Flight Sergeant Wilkes, a fellow captain and gallant friend. He was skilled, experienced and funny. Just before take-off on a delivery flight from Gibraltar with several Liberator pilots on-board who knew the hazards, he had reassured us with: 'It's all right, gentlemen, I've done this before.' He had, and it was.

Our night attacks on Tripoli and other North African targets soon became monotonous. Welcome and startling relief occurred during the westbound leg of a boring eight-hour flog. The night sky was suddenly illuminated by a long line of flashes to the left of us. Their origin proved to be the artillery fire that preceded the Eighth Army's final push westwards, which opened the way for the invasion of Italy.

The Army commander was General Montgomery. I had come across him in Cairo soon after he took over, when he lectured a bunch of junior Army officers – plus me, as a sort of fraternal extra. He electrified the soldiers by first telling them to ask themselves whether they were making themselves sufficiently offensive; and telling them, *inter alia*, that the only thing he would not tolerate was failure. A perturbing encounter.

As the Monty push gathered momentum, our attacks on the Wehrmacht bases became more intense and the Luftwaffe's opposition more effective. At a time of worrying losses we were visited by Marshal of the RAF, Lord Trenchard, the founding father of the RAF. He had lost none of his talent for building morale and cheering people up and praised us for the way we were doing a difficult and dangerous job. He also amused us with his advice to follow his example and live for twice as long after retirement as we had served. After retiring from the RAF he went on to take charge of the Metropolitan Police.

During this intensive phase the RAF 205 Group headquarters dispatched us to bomb Maleme, on the island of Crete. The raid was skilfully timed to prevent the moon from making it easy for the resident enemy fighters to intervene. One element in the plan that the dozy staff incredibly forgot was the sun, in the dawn light of which, in a disorganized gaggle, we were chased home across the Mediterranean. The appalling error made a transfer from the group's control a welcome change. Our new masters were the 98th Heavy Bombardment Group, US Army Air Corps, commanded by an American brigadier general called Timberlake. He evidently preferred the safety and comfort of his headquarters, never bothering to come to see us, not unlike the fellow senior officer subject to a ribald sailor's ditty:

> *Oh they tell us that the Admiral*
> *Is as nice as he can be,*
> *But we've never seen the Admiral*
> *Because the Admiral has never been to sea.*

On one of my final raids flak caused serious damage to one engine – not a great worry because the Liberator's feathering propellers gave it almost as good a performance on three engines as on four. We were short of fuel, however, and diverted to Fayid for an emergency landing. During our approach another engine failed and it was more than the combined efforts of two pilots could achieve to keep the aircraft straight. The resulting swing caused slight damage to a South African Air Force Spitfire parked close to the runway. The station commander drove out to the runway, to vent his fury on us, we feared. Not so. He welcomed what had happened because he expected that the damage would make the bolshie South Africans do what he had repeatedly asked – park the readiness fighter further from the end of the runway.

My last few raids were plagued by the winter weather typical of the Mediterranean. On a raid on the Tunisian port of Sousse it was so bad that we were lucky in being the only aircraft to find the target. At the nearby port of Sfax on another murky night, two of six bombs hit the quay, causing fires and explosions and much scurrying about. In the apparent absence of opposition I let down low, giving the delighted gunners the chance to strafe the warehouses, shipping and people. We returned for second and third helpings. During the departing climb, the top gunner, with a well-merited expletive, reported a barrage balloon. I remembered the Rugby wireless masts.

Sfax was my fiftieth raid, and I sensed a bothersome anxiety, well known and common in the much more demanding circumstances of bomber crews operating over Germany and defined as being 'operationally tired'. It was aggravated on my next two raids by heavy icing, lightning and St Elmo's fire silhouetting the guns and canopies in fluorescent blue light – boons because they grounded the fighters.

The weather had improved for my 53rd and last raid, which was an attack on Tripoli from 10,000 feet. We got away with a single run and good hits. In a fitting illuminated address, as I saw it, the searchlights gave me a farewell bath of light for an eternity of seconds before seeming to wave us away.

I got carried away – literally – by a troopship for the homeward voyage to Britain round the Cape of Good Hope, calling at Massawa, Port Sudan and Bombay. The ship was the converted liner *Mariposa*. For the next six weeks I was to share what had been a double first class cabin with seven US officers, amongst whom was a junior who had got into his university by virtue of his excellence as a footballer, an extroverted but agreeable major who had been a police officer in Pennsylvania, and an army doctor stricken with lung cancer who nevertheless chain-smoked.

The cabin was the only place to sit except on the decks, and even they were off limits during the ferociously enforced blackout. The food was excellent but served only twice a day, which made time hang even more heavily. It was altogether a trying journey.

My next disembarkation leave was a delight. I walked the Malvern Hills, at their best in the early spring, relishing my surroundings as they recovered their familiarity. Food was scarce but my mother did wonders at eking out the rations. I had time to reflect on how lucky I had been and how well I had been treated, especially during my years in the bomber business. Now, surfeited with *astra*, released from *ardua* and temporarily out of ardour, I was ready to comply with whatever might ensue.

Chapter 6

Home Skies

I had feared, metaphorically, running aground. In the event I could scarcely have been more pleased. I was posted to a flying job in the newly formed Transport Command at a station in Northern Ireland quaintly called Nutts Corner. I was to be an instructor at a new unit to train air crews, mainly from Bomber Command, for employment in civil aviation, familiarizing them with the Wellington enhanced with Pratt & Whitney Twin Wasp engines.

They were much more reliable and a joy to fly. Less joyful were some of the non-fliers. The station commander, Group Captain Roger Ford, was well known for letting others get on with their jobs and doing little himself. The adjutant, Flight Lieutenant Paul Hill, was highly competent but turned out to be a rogue. An exception to the motley collection was an attractive young clerical assistant, LAC, later Corporal, Rae Goodson. She worked for Squadron Leader John Bowie, a South African supposed to oversee the flying, and I used every excuse to visit her in her office. We soon got together, having picnic suppers on the Ulster hills, going to the cinema in Belfast, followed by dinner at the Carlton restaurant, well known for enormous steaks of dodgy provenance.

The flying, though not operational, was absorbing. I learnt as much as I taught, especially on the long cross-country navigation exercises done at night. Happily the route was a standard trip from Ireland across to St Abb's Head on the north-east coast of Scotland

and thence by way of St David's Head, on the south-west coast of Wales, and Chicken Rock, off the Isle of Man, and finally back to base. Knowing it well helped with putting errant student navigators back on the straight and narrow. For variety, I flew the Airspeed Oxford, not used for pilot training, as it had been at Cranwell, but as a runabout.

Rae had accepted my proposal, incidentally, at Belfast bus station, on a rainy night, and the Oxford came in handy for taking her to Malvern to meet my family. That trip was memorable for the adventurous return journey. The weather was terrible and I was obliged to fly as low as possible, creating a risk of hitting the Isle of Man. That didn't happen. But such was the turbulence that poor Rae was airsick. Not realizing that the ground crew were glad to clear up the results of this frequent occurrence at half a crown a time, she cleaned it up herself, using the clothes in her suitcase.

We were surprised and delighted by the award of the Distinguished Flying Cross for my work in the Middle East. The citation described how I had:

> made a number of daring attacks on Tobruk, Benghazi and later on Tripoli and carried out a daylight attack against shipping in the Mediterranean. On every occasion ... exhibited great perseverance and tenacity, remaining in the target area until certain of the results of the bombing. In December last, after delivering an effective attack on Sfax, he descended to 400 feet over the harbour to observe the results of his attack and obtained valuable information.

In retrospect I felt guilty about the unfairness to crews whose lives I had risked and who went unrewarded.

I was delighted in February 1944 to be posted to an operational transport squadron based at RAF Blakehill Farm in Wiltshire getting ready to take part in the invasion of Europe and get on with creating the long-awaited second front. The squadron, 233, was equipped with the Douglas Dakota DC3 (preceded by the DC2), whose versatility and superb quality as a beast of burden had been apparent since 1935. Over the years it had been variously configured, notably as a flying boat.

My fellow captains were a motley but distinguished bunch. The CO, Wing Commander Nigel Morrison, an ex-Cranwell cadet, was later to have the distinction of leading the very first stream of aircraft of the initial airborne assault on the French coast. Another ex-cadet, later a close friend, was Harry Jenkins. Amusing and super conscientious, he was dominated by a desire to emulate his father, a distinguished First World War pilot. Harry was at heart a field sportsman and naturalist, not really suited to being an airman, eventually retiring to his beloved Orkney.

My most interesting comrade was my flight commander, Geoff Lane, very bright and wonderfully funny, dashing frequently to London to take law exams. Forty years later, after a brilliant career at the bar, he became Lord Chief Justice of England. I came across him again when he gave a homily to a group of newly-appointed Assistant Recorders, including our elder son, David.

Rachel and I had planned to get married in late 1943. As it became obvious that there were familial reservations, we abandoned that plan. After putting it off again, we finally made it. To everybody's delight, the service took place at St Peter's Church in Vere Street, London. The reception was at the nearby De Vere hotel. The cake was tiered, as was usual, but the scarcity of ingredients was such that most of the layers were cardboard. We had asked for decorations that suited an air force couple and were galled to find that they were naval. We managed to get two days off for a honeymoon at Bramley Grange, a Surrey hotel. Rae and I remained together for more than sixty-seven years in marriage.

There soon arrived the source of another day off – a summons to a ceremony at Buckingham Palace, during which I would receive my DFC. We were all delighted that my father, who had been awarded the Order of the British Empire for his services to the Red Cross, was to receive his decoration at the same investiture. Far ahead of me in the queue because of the seniority of his award, he duly received his word of appreciation from King George VI. Just before he got to me, the king's aide de camp, an admiral, whispered a reminder that this was a father and son occasion. The king, suitably gracious, remarked on what a happy occasion it must be for us both. And it was for us all – particularly my father, who was so full of admiration for the RAF that he wrote a march called *Salute to the RAF*, which I still play on our piano.

Blakehill Farm expanded with the erection of a large tented transit camp for parachutists awaiting the advance of the invasion of Normandy. On one occasion two other senior pilots and I were invited to the camp mess for lunch. Whisky, which was scarce, flowed. After the meal, I found to my consternation that my car had been filled with petrol, at that time strictly rationed.

D-Day came a few days later and we were showered in messages of goodwill. Montgomery invoked the deity:

> The time has come to deal the enemy a terrific blow in Western Europe. Let us pray that 'The Lord Mighty in Battle' will aid us in the struggle.

A toe-curling assumption that God was on our side.

Chapter 7

Storming the European Ramparts

On 4 June the mighty invasion force was alerted for an assault that night. On the list of troops allotted to my aircraft I found William's name. My half-brother, William Collingwood, was then Brigade Major (pivot and general factotum) of the 3rd Parachute Brigade. I sought him out in the transit camp and we agreed that, for family reasons, he must go with someone else. The brigade commander readily agreed to a last-minute swap. After a day's delay because of bad weather, off we went.

The weather wasn't as good as all that. For success we needed a cloud base of not less than 700 feet with decent visibility underneath, and that was what we got. We were soon over the dropping zone. To my dismay, one poor man failed to jump before it became too dangerous. He begged for another chance. I let down from 600 to 400 feet and flew over the zone again.

Meanwhile, William had suffered a misfortune and a misadventure. The misfortune was being assigned to an Armstrong Whitworth Albemarle – a ghastly aircraft. It was said in jest that the 600 supplied to the RAF were constructed in steel and wood by the Times Furnishing Company, made, as the mail order catalogues put it, for simple home assembly. The misadventure was that the aircraft from which he was supposed to drop was hit as it approached the dropping zone. As he jumped, complete with vital documents and a 60lb kit bag, his release strop jammed. He was left dangling in the ether as the aircraft turned to return to base. As the crew hauled him back inside they dislocated his hip. Desperate to get back to France because of the documents, he managed to get a lift in a glider of the Airlanding Brigade. The brigade commander later described what followed:

> On D+1 who should hobble into my headquarters but Bill Collingwood, with his dislocated hip sticking out sideways. Unfortunately you could not have a semi-crippled brigade major and thirty-six hours later the medics took him away. What an extraordinary feat of mental endurance and guts that was.

All he got was an MBE – a sadly junior Membership of the Order of the British Empire. But it added to the family score: the OBE for my father and CBE for me (and one later for our elder son).

After the launch and follow-up there were two unexplained and irksome days of inaction. The reason soon became clear. It was that the planners had allowed for many more casualties than there were. It was as discomfiting to realize that we were meant to be dead as it was relieving to get back on the job as all-purpose carriers for the forces with a foothold in France. As the foothold became firmly established, the Royal Engineers, with lightning speed, used PSP (Pierced Steel Planking) to create the landing strips that enabled us to advance, airfield by airfield, into France and later Germany. On the return flights we carried casualties, who were attended to by excellent nursing orderlies. They were landed at an airfield equipped to receive them where Rachel was stationed. She was one of the team of carers who looked after them, sometimes on long ambulance journeys to hospital.

Rachel and I found digs at a farmhouse in Cricklade, a village between the two airfields – Down Ampney and Blakehill Farm – at which she and I were respectively based.

Back at work, I was ashamed to learn of the poor result of the D-Day drop. Many of the parachutists had landed far from their planned destinations and the brigade commander, Brigadier James Hill, had the daunting task of regrouping them into battle formation. Some of our young crews' lack of steadiness under fire was probably a contributory factor, of which I and other seniors felt ashamed. (Hill became a lifelong friend and president of the brigade memorial association, greatly revered and respected by the French. In his late eighties he finally had to give up and handed over the presidency to me.)

The summer wore on and the Allies' advance slowed. General Eisenhower, Supreme Commander of the Allied forces in Europe, saw a way of regaining the momentum. The US 82nd Airborne Division were to land in central Holland near Njemegen, not far ahead of the main land force. The British 1st Airborne Division, at the bidding of General Montgomery, had as its objective the bridge over the river Waal at Arnhem. That was a bold, perhaps reckless, stroke because the main force front line, west of Utrecht, was a long way west of the Waal.

I took part in the Arnhem drop, feeling that 233 Squadron, well knit after three months together and in action, would acquit itself better than the undertrained, unseasoned unit that had stumbled on D-Day. For the launch I had a fully loaded glider in tow. The lumbering take-off reminded me of my struggles on hot afternoons at Fayid. It was soon apparent that all was not well at Arnhem because Montgomery's main force was taking unexpectedly long to catch up. Four days after the launch we were asked for a maximum effort to replenish the main force, now contained within a small perimeter round the Waal Bridge. I carried sixteen 350lb panniers of petrol and ammunition.

The dispatchers, soldiers of the Royal Army Service Corps as it was then, did their job wonderfully in a single run over the dropping zone. That was a relief because the anti-aircraft fire was the thickest I had ever seen and the Dakota casualties were high. One reason, we later discovered, was that the German anti-aircraft guns had been augmented with field artillery elevated skywards. Together they were firing at the predictable line of approach we were forced to follow.

Even that frightening task was not without light relief. As we sped away our regular dispatcher, an Irish RASC private, shouted from the plastic dome that was the sole way of seeing behind: 'Bandits!' – the code for fighters about to attack. We had taught him the standard way of reporting their whereabouts – port, starboard beam, quarter, ahead, astern, high, low. Nothing but silence followed his shout. The awful gap seemed so long and worrying that I asked, 'Come on, Paddy, where are they?' After a further aeon of seconds came the answer: 'There's hunderts of the buggers.' By then I was corkscrewing close to the ground, making the fighters' task nearly impossible and once again we were spared anything but a few bullet holes.

Two days later came the same again. I was leading the formation behind with panniers of petrol and ammunition. The anti-aircraft fire was intense but no worse than before, but mishaps at the back of my aircraft meant that it took three terrifying runs over the target zone to get rid of the load. It was a great relief to dive away, this time free from marauding fighters. But it was galling to learn later that the dropping zone was at least partly in German hands.

Three missions, the middle one of which I had missed, took a terrible toll. Flight Lieutenant David Lord, of Down Ampney, despite having his aircraft hit and set on fire, carried on with his run and delivered his load before crashing, killing all aboard. He was awarded a posthumous Victoria Cross. Other awards included an immediate DSO, five DFCs, one bar to a DFC (mine), a US Air Medal and a US DFC.

For the time being we carried on, literally and figuratively, as before. As the numbers of the 'B' landing grounds increased we entered the removal business, shifting whole fighter squadrons and their effects from airfields in Britain to the Continent, sometimes reassured by the presence of their aircraft as escorts. Returning with a load of casualties after one such move I saw, well below and some way on our port side, what looked like a fighter with flame issuing from its back end. It reminded me of the primordial jet I had seen at Cranwell. I broke radio silence to report the possibility of an imminent attack, but nothing materialized. At home that evening I heard the news of the arrival and explosion in a field of the first of the V-1s, powered missiles that caused much damage during the next few months.

By now I had begun to feel some of the despondency and exhaustion that had afflicted me in the Middle East. There would, I felt, be more Arnhems and our casualties would be high, even in comparison with our comrades in Bomber Command. In what could have been defiance, I applied for a permanent commission in the RAF. At about the same time came another task. I was to be part of yet another enormous force, now known as the 1st Allied Airborne Army, for the final assault on Germany. After three days at a semi-derelict airfield at Birch, near Colchester, I towed a glider across the Rhine at Wesel in the company of all the aircraft available and a huge American DC3 armada to the south. We had all apprehended another bloody encounter, but compared with Arnhem, opposition to the Rhine was slight; 233 Squadron's losses were nil and there were said to have been only nineteen aircraft destroyed out of a force exceeding 1,000. Our aircraft fuel tanks had suffered bullet holes, fortunately non-incendiary. Along with several other Dakotas incontinent of fuel, we littered B57, the airfield at Nivelles, near Brussels, where nuns from a nearby convent offered us peaches and booze.

Rachel had been upset by being told that I had been reported missing, but was reassured soon afterwards.

Chapter 8

In for the Long Haul

As the Allied domination of Europe became complete, we began the job of ferrying ever-growing numbers of liberated Allied prisoners of war home to Britain, cramming thirty-plus of these emaciated men into a compartment meant for no more than twenty. My record was thirty-eight. I remember particularly a wounded colonel who had concealed a bottle of brandy under his blanket, no doubt for a celebration when he got home. Unwashed, in threadbare uniform, they wolfed the Dundee cake they were offered and were promptly sick. We took them to a specially adapted airfield at Wing, near Aylesbury, where they were deloused, cleaned and, as they deserved, well spoilt.

During and after VE-Day we conducted business as usual. Unusually, I was required to go on a confidential mission to B156, the German airfield at Luneberg, where one of the surrenders had taken place. The job turned out to be to collect no fewer than nineteen German generals and a colonel, plus a well-armed escort. They were to be delivered to Croydon, the pre-war civil airport for London, undulating and devoid of runways. The captives were docile and we were polite except for one general, ignorant of quarantine rules, who protested at being deprived of his *kleine hund* (little dog). Lassie didn't come home.

In mid-June 1945, 233 Squadron had itself to move to Odiham, an old-established permanent station but, like Croydon, uneven and all grass. It had as a runabout an Auster, a puddle-jumper meant for light reconnaissance for the Army; and, nostalgically, another Oxford. Both were fun to fly. The station commander was bachelor Group Captain John Simpson, the subject of the Hector Bolitho biography *Combat Report*, which I had reviewed. I was saddened that the booze had taken its toll. After what passed for work, John's invariable habit was to repair to the officers' mess, where he drank whisky until closing time. Closing time was when he, fit only to be shepherded to bed, said it was. He astonished everybody by proposing to Gillie Potter, the chief WAAF officer. They married amidst much alcoholic celebration. Rachel and I were very concerned about Gillie, a dear friend. There proved to be ample cause. Very sadly, John shot himself a few years afterwards in Green Park, having left a suicide note with the barman at Shepherds, a flashy Mayfair pub. Our sadness for Gillie, with whom we kept in touch until she died in the 1990s, was infinite.

The work load lessened and we soon found out why. The squadron was to move again, this time to the Far East, where, of course, the war continued. Our hearts sank at the prospect of a two-year separation, but they soon surfaced again when, because of two overseas tours I had already done, I was deemed ineligible for another.

My new posting was another pleasant surprise. I had felt sure that I would have to go to a ground job. Instead, I was to join, as a flight commander, another Dakota squadron, 525, at RAF Membury, in the middle of nowhere on the Wiltshire Downs. (The name was later preserved as that of the nearby motorway services stop.) The squadron commander was Wing Commander Roy Dutton, a Battle of Britain pilot who I came to know well.

Just as we moved into digs near Marlborough, to my amazement and delight I heard that, being amongst the first twenty or so applicants, I had been awarded a permanent commission.

Squadron 525's role was long-range transport, in which I revelled. Malta, usually our first stop, had an opera house whence came tintinnabulating morsels of *La Traviata*, and *Cav* and *Pag* (the short operas *Cavalleria Rusticana* and *Pagliacci*, usually performed together). The delights of the Floriana Gut – the haunt of sin that had amused me years before – were still to be enjoyed.

Iraq boasted the best station in the RAF – Habbaniyah – where every known sport, polo included, was to be had. To arrive there after a boiling hot progression along the desert pipeline from Cairo that doubled as a navigational aid, was to have reached Nirvana. On one occasion, during a post-flight aircrew meal, I felt faint. A doctor sitting opposite urged me to drink water with plenty of salt in it to replace the salt in my sweat. Almost instantly, I felt better.

We used Habbaniya as a 'slip' stop, giving crews a day's interval before taking on the next aircraft to arrive. Next came either Sharjah or Bahrein, both almost devoid of facilities other than fuel. That didn't stop some idiot from asking that the slip should be shifted from Habbaniya to either of the latter two to make the trip less exhausting. Our easternmost stop was at Allahabad; those hoping for the glamours and amours of the Orient were dismayed to find themselves in a spotless boarding house run by the draconian widow of a British civil servant of the Raj. She locked the doors at ten, willy-nilly, as that practice might very aptly be described.

As a flight commander I could pick and choose my trips. One I kept for myself. Every Sunday, very early, I flew a load of newspapers to RAF Bückeburg in Germany. Amidst the big bundles were two complete sets of all the papers. One was for General Montgomery, still commanding the 21st Army Group, who had cropped up at various stages of my RAF career. The other bundle was for me. At home Rachel and I gorged ourselves on the prurient rubbish. Her pregnancy was going well and, great with child, she went to Malvern, where my father kept an eye on her. He asked his favourite gynaecological colleague to deliver. He did: to our boundless joy, a boy.

Chapter 9

Domestic Interlude

Before I could finish my tour I found myself posted to what I had been lucky enough to avoid for the whole war and, until then, for the peace – a ground job. I could hardly complain. In the air the trivial round, the common task, as an Ancient and Modern hymn puts it, had finished all I needed to ask – and a great deal more. Now came the time for something completely different.

I became a founder member of the new RAF Selection Board. Its job was to conduct tests on aspiring candidates for Cranwell cadetships and permanent commissions. The president was Air Commodore George Beamish, scion of a famous Irish Family also comprising: two fighter pilots, Charles and Victor (the latter killed in the Battle of Britain); Cecil, a dental officer with whom I later served in the Far East; and a formidable WAAF sister. George was funny and kind. He had conducted the evacuation of the RAF from Crete in 1941 with great distinction, but seniority had kept him from aircrew operations, at which he would undoubtedly have distinguished himself. He retired as an air marshal, later standing as a Tory candidate for Belfast, to the amused stupefaction of all who knew him, and, to their unsurprised regret, failing.

The rest of us were a cross-section of the RAF emerging from the war. Beamish's deputy was Group Captain Paul Holder, exactly right as the brains to complement George's brawn. Down one level were the wing commanders David Evans, William Nicholas and David Scott Malden. William Nicholas was a former Halton apprentice who became an air gunner with an excellent record in Bomber Command (unsurprisingly, because of the careful selection and excellent training given to apprentices). David Scott Malden was a very successful Battle of Britain pilot with an intellect of great depth, tragically to die of lung disease a few years later. The rest were 'lowly' squadron leaders. One beside me was John Preston, an RAF fencing champion, and Lawrence Reavell-Carter, a shot-putter blessed with native wit. He had shown his stamina and guts as one of the heroic escapers who had survived the shooting of forty comrades as, with sixty others, they escaped through a tunnel from a German prisoner of war camp. Another veteran of Bomber Command, festooned with decorations earned from multiple raids over Europe, was Roger Reece, a man of great modesty, which was later apparent when he took holy orders. Subsidiary advisers included an RAF consultant psychiatrist and a civilian polymath, Maurice Backett, later to come my way as a professor concerned with medical training and health education.

As I was buckling down to an unfamiliar job, our family was stricken by my father's death at sixty-seven. His health had been failing for months, struggling with great fortitude to look after his patients while suffering with what he called cardiac asthma – akin, as I understood it, to emphysema. Its origin was probably twofold – cigarette smoking and the gassings he had endured during a period of gallant service commanding a field ambulance for four years during the First World War, service for which he was awarded a Distinguished Service Order, an unusual decoration for a doctor.

When his final illness began, I helped my mother to find a *locum tenens* to look after the practice. He turned out to be a newly demobilized RAF doctor in the rank of wing commander. He at once took to the work, but found the burden that my father had been carrying for years almost more than he could cope with. He was so impressed that he bought the practice and the house, where he stayed until his retirement twenty years later. My father survived long enough to see David, our elder son, but sadly died before the christening.

In common with other family events, the christening service was conducted by a lifelong family friend, the Reverend George Snow. I first met him at Charterhouse, where he was a popular and highly successful teacher and chaplain. He later married the kind and hospitable Joan, whom we had met when George became headmaster of Ardingly. They had three sons, including Jon, the television broadcaster.

The selection board started in a large country house at Framewood Manor, which had been requisitioned for the duration of the war. The owner had been content to leave it as a useful source of income, but suddenly wanted it back. We moved the board to another country house, this time of full stately status, near Ascot and Sunningdale. Sunninghill Park had magnificent grounds and a lake with a bridge into which resident swans, belying their reputation as good aviators, often crashed on alighting. The house and out-buildings offered excellent facilities and our work prospered. It was to select as much of the cream of Britain's youth as the RAF could attract, candidates for Cranwell – back in business much as it had been before the war but with the great advantage of a more catholic field of choice. We were also charged with selecting officers from those who had asked for their short service commissions to be made permanent.

We used practical tests with logs, planks and bricks, usually involving some form of contrivance and absorbing enough for candidates to forget themselves and help the watching testers to distinguish the pushy from the diffident and the bright from the dim. There were discussions in small groups and in plenary session, and interviews decreasing in length with the seniority of the interviewer. The candidates were put into numbered overalls to promote literal uniformity and secure anonymity. At the end of the four-day cycle we reviewed all we had learnt of each candidate at length, not looking at other sources such as school reports until we had reached consensus. We ended by classifying candidates in suitability for cadetships or commissions in categories A to F (plus an unofficial self-explanatory extra F to OMDB, meaning only acceptable Over My Dead Body – in case of benefit-of-the-doubt tendencies at senior level).

There was much interest from on high. One VIP visitor was Air Chief Marshal Sir John Slessor, a former bomber pilot, an intellectual and, most rare in that exalted category, a likeable and modest man. His reaction was to thank his lucky stars that he had got his permanent commission by having an uncle in the War Office. In diametric contrast was Air Marshal Sir Basil Embry, Commander-in-Chief of Fighter Command and an exemplar of what were known as the Barons – very senior office holders who paid little heed to the dicta of the Air Ministry. His notorieties included wasting, in defiance of authority, a huge sum of public money on blast walls round all the individual aircraft hard standings in his command, subsequently shown to be almost useless. His alternative to our selection process, he told us not entirely in jest, perhaps, would be to lock all the candidates in one room and commission the survivors.

I found my family rooms in the servants' quarters of a mansion with a large garden that shared a fence with the Golden Gates of Ascot racecourse. Our co-tenants were the Deputy President Group Captain Paul Holder, his charming wife, Betty, and their young family. The house, belonging to an ancient admiral with a VC, was lit solely by carbide gas generated in one of the garages and piped into the rooms. The only heating was from fires. Almost at once the notoriously cold winter of 1946–47 set in and, in spite of a doctor's certificate for a priority supply of coal to keep three small children warm, neither Paul nor I could get any, the local merchant's yard being bare. Fortunately, there was an abandoned timber-hutted former American military camp in the Selection Board's grounds opposite our front gate. Paul and I, with hammers, jemmy and cross-cut saw, spent most of our free time before and after work dismantling the huts and sawing the product into foot-long bits of wood, which sufficed to keep us warm throughout the terrible seven-week freeze-up. The work afforded wonderful exercise and the leisurely hours of our jobs meant that the task was not too onerous.

Like those of Framewood Manor, Sunninghill Park's RAF days were numbered. The trouble this time was that it had been chosen as an out-of-town residence for the then Princess Elizabeth and her husband, Prince Philip. The Board, having learnt lessons in mobility from the first upheaval, soon re-established itself at Ramridge House, near Andover, again commodious and pleasant.

Reavell-Carter and I, roped in to ensure that the Board's departure for Ramridge left Sunninghill in good order, were taking a final look round to ensure that all was well just after noon, handing-over time on the appointed day. Suddenly, a large Rolls-Royce drew up alongside us. The passenger was King George VI in the uniform of a marshal of the RAF. Reminding us of the time, he asked brusquely why we were still in occupation.

'Because, Sire,' said Reavell-Carter, never at a loss, 'we want to be doubly sure that all is in the good order in which you would wish to find it.' Mollified, the king wished us well and moved on.

Our efforts were wasted. The Ministry of Works, into whose care the house was to be handed for refurbishment, had been told of the elaborate fire precautions RAF units always took, featuring airmen detailed in turn as fire picket on twenty-four-hour patrol at short intervals all round the premises, and of the particular hazard of fissures in the timber window frames, currently having the old paint off them, creating a need for special vigilance. The Ministry, studiedly rude, knew better: the house went up in flames forty-eight hours later. I remembered that RAF routine included the issue of an anti-fire poster whose standard message ended with: 'In the event of the fire being too large for the finder to deal with ...' the remaining space being left for any local provisions that unit commanders might think appropriate. Almost invariably there appeared the scrawled waggery: 'look for a smaller one.'

Housing in rural Hampshire was plentiful. We soon took up residence in yet another set of servants' quarters, again very spacious, on the top floor of a neo-Georgian mansion in the hamlet of Tangley. The original owner's widow and her handicapped daughter still lived in the grand parts. We got on well: among other favours we did them was looking after, in their absence, the noisy flock of guinea fowl – admirable guard birds.

To ease Rachel's burden of child care we invested in a nanny – a girl of sixteen. She ate a great deal and spent an inordinate amount of time having baths, swallowing both the water and the time she could have spent nannying. We cooked on a large Valor oil stove, never reliable and subject to panic attacks. One struck as we cooked a leg of lamb for a supper party: the indulgent guests valiantly scraped the black grease off their helpings. We were also afflicted with mice until I hit upon an inspired solution: a cat.

After just under a year at Ramridge I felt increasing boredom and the urge to get back to flying: an RAF unit without aircraft being every bit as lonesome and drear, as the ditty has it, as a pub without beer. I had also been troubled by one of the criteria applied to our candidates and often the theme of discussions: 'Identification with the service.' The people we wanted must have their hearts and souls in the RAF, ran the argument: it could never be enough to remain no more than a contracted employee, however bright and efficient. Reflecting on that point, I realized that my own stance was really no more than that of a contractor: in it for the flying. That, I see in retrospect, was the first zephyr of an emotional gale that eventually blew me into civil life.

Chapter 10

Buttoned Up and Flying Right

With insight typical of him, Sir John Slessor had seen the merit of bringing together the younger of the pilots chosen for commissions and putting them through a specially enhanced instructor's course at the Central Flying School (CFS). Several such courses were arranged and I was to be put on one of them. After some refresher flying, I found myself before a board of senior CFS staff curious to discover what sort of clay was to be thrown on their collective potter's wheel. Interviewing me, the cheerful chief instructor asked, 'When did you last show your arse to the Lord?'

No such display, I had to admit, had occurred since the brief aerobatic sessions with David Bamford that had so excited me at Sywell. That, he assured me, would soon be put right. It was.

Under various guiding hands but mostly with the deft and sagacious Canadian instructor of instructors, Peter Johnson, I learnt the professional way of doing the quasi-instructional work I had taken to at Nutts Corner and later done in a supervisory way in 233 and 525 Squadrons. I made friends with the Harvard single-engined trainer. Built in America in thousands as the AT-6 and the mainstay of most pilot training, the Harvard had a Pratt & Whitney Wasp engine – wonderfully reliable but with the single disadvantage of a deafeningly noisy propeller. Gradually mastering the technique of flying it properly from the rear of its in-line cockpits and endlessly practising aerobatics with the long-suffering Johnson, I finished the six-month course as a half-decent instructor.

My pleasure was enhanced by the extra type-flying that the Slessor add-ons had provided. I got my hands on the Percival Prentice, an airborne greenhouse, and this time I exploited its renowned manoeuvering and aerobatic qualities to the full. There was the acme of versatility, the Mosquito, admirable as an advanced trainer and no less so in light bombing, night fighting and transport. To my great joy there was the Spitfire, every bit as docile and nimble as I had been led to expect, and at the opposite end of the gamut of fame, the Lancaster, mainstay of the post-Wellington generation of bombers and as rough and rudimentary as the Liberator had been smooth and elaborate. All in all, my flying was transformed, finishing what Sywell, Cranwell and Harwell had started.

All of this was as nothing compared with the birth, just as the course ended, of our second son, Gregor. Rachel had gone to her family home in Glastonbury when we left Tangley and had the baby at the cottage hospital at Butleigh on the adjoining Somerset levels. Far from being present at the birth, I was at the time doing a low-level solo cross-country flight over the wilds of Wales in a Harvard. The CFS controller had trouble in getting the news to me because the mountains got in the way.

Now a multi-role instructor of the B1 grade, I was bursting for a chance to put my new skill to work. It soon came. I was to return to the RAF College Cranwell, joining the advanced flying squadron on the Harvard.

One point of piquancy was that the cadets were the young men who had passed through the selection processes, affording me the interest of seeing how they turned out. Another was that George Beamish had also been posted to Cranwell as Air Officer Commanding over the clutch of units based there and Commandant of the College. George, usually brusque, could be charming and amusing; one instance was his habit of lining up the children alongside the saluting base for the cadets' march past after church parade. He was determined to keep in with local bigwigs, glad when kindnesses were reciprocated and interested in cadets' leisure activities. One such kindness came from a local mine owner who from time to time entertained cadets and showed them round his mine. Unaware that two cadets returning to the college on a rainy afternoon carrying golf bags had been entertained in this way, he asked them the silly question as to whether they had been playing golf. On receiving the reply, 'No, Sir, we've been down a coal mine,' his pink complexion turned to purple at what he thought was an insolent piece of sarcasm. Happily, he soon calmed down enough to accept the young men's explanation.

Restored to pre-war status and with a syllabus aspiring to equate with that of a university, the college could hardly have differed more from its wartime guise. From an instructor's standpoint, not all the changes were to the good. One snag was the time sunk into marching to the resident band, far superior to the wartime fife and drum combination but not above rendering the *Lincolnshire Poacher* with preliminary obbligato and the enhanced *Colonel Bogey* of my cadet days. There was much ancillary education grouped under the weird title 'Humanistics'. Demanding obeisance from all else was sport. Both diluted flying training. The result was a running dispute and a sort of class distinction between ourselves, the horny-handed flying instructor technicians down at the airfield, and the polished, cultured beings gracing the college headed by the housemaster 'act-alikes' known as cadet wing officers, there to instil what would really count towards successful careers. One such, entirely atypical, was Harry Jenkins, back from Burma, potency restored and nesting happily with Marion. Harry's presence lubricated relations between the horny-handed and the elite. But the hegemony of the Assistant Commandant and the Director of Studies, the latter somewhere between a headmaster and vice-chancellor, made training cadets to fly much harder than it was at ordinary flying training schools.

We humble toilers were expected to join the gilded college staff on such occasions as the formal dinner in the large, long-tabled hall. Those of us keen to get home would sit near the bottom end and, when there was a moment of diversion such as a speech, crawl under the table to the end, darting thence to the nearest door. But there was no escaping the drill sessions preparatory to the passing-out

51

parades that culminated each course. As some compensation we could use the superb sports facilities and, to great benefit, the cadet education staff, who were a great help in preparing for the newly restored promotion and staff college exams.

Life in this setting was none too easy for those of us with young families and in housing well short of luxurious. We had moved into a roomy flat in a small Georgian manor house in Leasingham, 6 miles equidistant from the college and Sleaford, the shopping town. The lady of the manor was a young widow.

We didn't stay there long. A benevolent Air Ministry, concerned at the plight of young married officers, abandoned the appalling pre-war distinction between the 'qualified' married officers and the 'unqualified', whose much lower allowances kept them in penury. The Ministry even went so far as to introduce a disturbance allowance of £20, payable every time a domestic move took place after a qualifying period of six months.

Like most of my cash-starved brothers in arms, I joined a sort of general post every six months and one day. This time, the result was our grandest home so far – a bungalow in a quiet road in the village of Ruskington, where I first fell in love with vegetable growing. When we were succeeded as tenants by a navigator, who shall be nameless, his reply to my question about making use of the veg was that he hadn't even bothered to go into the garden. Opposite lived another instructor, Dennis Bedford, and his wife Stella. The soul of kindness, Dennis rescued me from the tyranny of country buses by driving me to and from Cranwell. I would rather have paddled my own canoe or, rather, driven my Morris 8 or ridden my own motorbike, but I had had to sell them both to save up for school fees.

Smarting from the average assessment I had received on passing out of CFS, I put in for a re-categorization test during the forthcoming six-monthly visit from the CFS examining team. After a frantic brush-up of my aerobatics by John Gibbons, expert in that craft and a good friend, I was tested in the air by the naval member of the team, a notoriously hard man. He, I blush to record, was favourably impressed, describing my flow of verbiage during a simulated flying lesson as 'Churchillian' and complimenting me on an error-free ground test. He awarded me the next upward category, A2, and the norm that competency with experience could expect to achieve. In contrast, I got into trouble for inveighing against the needless disruption of his training caused to one of my cadets, John Danton, who had sustained a boxing injury that kept him on the ground. The trouble was worthwhile because it almost certainly contributed to the ban on cadets boxing.

By now a flight commander, I had fewer cadets and more time. Some of it I devoted to teaching gliding in a T21 trainer, and thus preparing cadets who had volunteered to take part in the annual gliding camp at a mountain site at Scharfollendorf in Germany. Another diversion was parading with the glossy college staff in rehearsing and taking part in the passing out parades.

On one of these, dolled up in my best blue and polished to the nines, I stood last in a line of supernumerary officers (i.e. surplus to the flight and squadron commanders but adding an extra row to the ranks of cadets). We were all waiting for the order to march past that would end the dreadful half-hour or so of standing still while the visiting bigwig did his or her inspection with little chats to randomly chosen lads. I was close to the venerated queen's colour – a blue silk embroidered flag on an ornate pole, attended by a colour party and held aloft by the tallest cadet on the course. He was in our flight and his name was Mullarkey (yes, really). I noticed with alarm that his normal healthily pink complexion had turned pale grey and the colour was gently swaying. Breaching the requirement to stand stock still, I motioned to the magisterial college warrant officer who had, as it were, a roving non-commission on the parade. This lantern-jawed martinet with a heart of gold, George Millis, acting as if he were executing some part of the parade liturgy, marched stiffly across to Mullarkey and stood behind him with his hands in his armpits. He delivered, *sotto voce*, a homily on the consequential effects on his career of any variation from the vertical. The oscillation lessened and just before the order to march, Mullarkey's face changed colour for the better. I prided myself with the reflection that they also serve who only stand and wait; especially if they keep their eyes open and their wits about them.

My luck held. I was posted from Cranwell to the Central Flying School (CFS) Examining Wing as a squadron commander. From the standards of flying and examining, it was clear what a much better pilot I would have to become and how much there was to learn. Profiting greatly from the help of my colleagues, I tried to raise my standard of instrument flying to a point that would qualify me as an instrument rating as well as an instructional technique examiner. After one failure I succeeded, and at once started on the weekly grind of visits to flying training schools throughout the RAF and the Fleet Air Arm, as well as advanced training units, using single-engined aircraft: a formidable parish.

The other squadron, commanded by another former Cranwell instructor and family friend, Dick Wakeford, covered multi-engined training. In due course we became largely interchangeable. We had in our unit commander by far the best senior officer I ever encountered, Wing Commander John Barraclough. He was later to become very senior and the object of universally recognized excellence. He was full of wit and humour but sensitive in his dealings with all sorts of people. He was contemptuous of higher authority, almost visibly struggling to conceal what he thought of the CFS commandant at the time. Preparing for the annual ceremony of the parade and inspection by the Air Officer Commanding, John realized that his shoes were far from up to snuff. He borrowed a new pair from the only examiner who shared his size, Flight Lieutenant Bert Slade, lending Bert his own shoes in exchange. As the inspecting party approached our serried ranks, John stopped in front of Bert and delighted the rest of us with a solemn warning to him never to appear on parade so badly shod again. As an excellent pilot and a natural leader, John epitomized the component of the RAF officer corps that did most to win the war: not the polished Cranwell product, good as it was, but the unemployed bank clerks of the 1930s, as they had been unkindly typified, who got short service commissions. John had started life as a Stock Exchange junior.

At the end of our teams' weekly visits of inspection we reviewed our findings with the chief instructor of the unit and usually the station commander. John would often fly up in our runabout Avro Anson to attend the review. After one such visit to Cranwell, as we were flying home he remarked of an aristocratically named group captain: 'Married again? This time it's a scrumptious bit of South American crumpet, his third or fourth; I think he just wears them out.' At that moment we both realized that the internal intercom system on which we had been chatting was also in external mode, broadcasting all he had said over a big slice of middle England. From other aircraft came such catcalls as, 'Oh my!' and 'Get him,' with other less printable ribaldry.

Chapter 11

Glimpses of the Orient

The weekly visits were interspersed with training sessions at Little Rissington, which made for some sort of home life. But my absences were taxing for Rachel and the boys, especially while we were housed in a small, draughty cottage in the hamlet of Maugersbury, down the hill from Stow-on-the-Wold. But it was blessed with a small, safe garden, and there was a good first school for David in Stow. Everything improved when we were allotted an RAF house on the airfield. On the patch, as it was called, there was plenty of company and help of all kinds.

The new neighbours were a boon to Rachel during our periods of absence overseas to a miscellany of RAF and foreign units. For the first one that I did, under John Barraclough, we borrowed a Dakota with a cream-walled interior, a carpeted floor and blue leather armchairs. We were allowed to borrow this 'tarted up for VIPs' model thanks to inspired wangling by John and his friends in high places. Most of the route I had crossed and re-crossed over the years, especially in 525 Squadron. But this time we took in Ceylon (later Sri Lanka), where there was still an RAF base at Negombo (later Katunayake), reputedly the most beautiful airfield in the world with its sand-coloured surface, palms and fresh greenery. Guam, I later decided, just beat it. There we flew the elderly resident Harvards, testing the pilots of the small detachment, egregious in starched bush jackets in a special off-khaki shade, and their

Sinhalese charges. In crumpled shirts on licence from mothballed drawers at home, we looked like tropical scarecrows. On the way eastwards we refuelled at the holiday brochure resort of Car Nicobar, later visiting the RAF bases at Changi and Tengah on Singapore Island and the still primitive hutted base at Butterworth on the Malayan mainland opposite Penang Island.

There I was landed, in two senses. I was asked to test a sergeant pilot thought to be unsafe, having somehow passed through the training system without being rumbled. We took off in a Mosquito happily enough and I spent an hour or so on hot and exhausting dual re-instruction. The session went well and I had thoughts of a successful salvage job. To build up his confidence we did a single-engined approach with one engine feathered, an excellent source of self-reassurance, not unduly dangerous if a safe approach speed was maintained but offering almost no possibility of going round again. In the late stages of the approach the sergeant panicked, freezing on the controls as we sank towards Nemesis. My own panic gave me strength as, overriding him, I gave the good engine as much get-out-of-trouble thrust as I dared and we just made it over the airfield boundary. Home he went.

Our Far East extremity, reached via a refuelling stop at Saigon, was Kai Tak, the RAF base in Hong Kong. All the pilots' instrument ratings, in effect, licences to fly in bad weather, had run out and we slaved to requalify them, glad to depart for overnight stops in Thailand, Burma and the Indian Air Force base at Calcutta, still with its Raj base of Dum Dum. There were glimpses of the glamour of the Orient, sort of. One was the famous Nai Yang night club in Bangkok, with a chorus line whose legs, unencumbered with underwear, had skirts that would have struck their occidental sisters as wanting. John resolved to return some time to look at their faces. A more sedate feature was the beautiful Schwedagon Pagoda, its graceful gold-leafed tower gleaming in the sun as we made for Mingaladon, a landmark in the war in Burma. Rivalling the pagoda as we refuelled at Palam, the airport for Delhi, was the exquisite white marble Taj Mahal (the latter word being the source of the horrid word 'mall', as in shopping).

The last major stop was at the Royal Pakistan Air Force base at Risalpur, near Quetta, a town well known to old stagers as the home of the alternative, allegedly soft option, British Army Staff College. Most of Risalpur's CFS-trained instructors were well up to standard, re-categorizing successfully in their ancient Harvards and Tiger Moths. So also were the cadets, free from most of the trammels of their opposite numbers. I was surprised at the strength of patriotic feeling manifest in the demand, absurd in an English-speaking country, for a translation of the famous CFS pilot training manual into Urdu.

Off duty, to a degree, we had to endure formal guests that out-Cranwelled Cranwell with its stiff routine, terrible mess games, over copious whisky and absence of any chance of escaping under the table. The best part of the other hospitality consisted in a fascinating day tour of the North-West Frontier with Afghanistan. The road ran through mountains adorned with huge stone replicas of crests of the British Army regiments that had defended the frontier for so long. So fixed, in those days, were the defences that the emplacements of the machine-gun companies are listed in the classic *Imperial Military Geography* by Major (later Brigadier) Cole, studied by generations of would-be staff college students, me included. At one stop there were tribesmen armed with the home-made rifles that Kipling wrote about; though whether they were akin to the moth-eaten Highlanders stationed at car parks in the Scottish Highlands for tourists to photograph was not free from doubt. Westering home along the familiar route, I, as the only Dakota-qualified pilot other than John, was glad to share with him the completion of an onerous trip that had tired us all out.

Chapter 12

On the Wing

Now began the first of the three parts of my flying career that compete for the title 'The Time of my Life' (the others being the Dakota and the Vulcan periods). Especially enjoyable were the next two of our six-monthly visits to the Rhodesian Air Training Group, kept in being there because of the cost savings that the flawless weather made possible. For the first time I had the company of John Barraclough's successor, Wing Commander Russell Bell, a Royal Australian Air Force officer who later transferred to the RAF. Understandably, he found John a hard act to follow. Unqualified as an instructor, he had been on the staff of the RAF Flying College, a recently established advanced training unit for senior officers. He neither liked nor understood basic flying training, and he was also irascible.

My flight commander and long-term friend, Norman Smith, had a widower father who had had the classic misfortune of being grabbed by a predatory widow. Norman asked me to take his place on one of his week-long visits so that he could help with and go to the wedding. When we asked Bell to approve the change he petulantly asked why. Norman's 'So that I can be best man at my father's wedding,' did not commend itself as a reply; we both had trouble in figuratively hosing him down.

Qualified on the Dakota (this time a standard model), Bell flew some of the legs of the journey. But such help did not make up for his irritable conduct at the destinations and week-long visits to the training schools at Heany, near Bulawayo and Thornhill, near Gwelo, in the copper belt. The routine was the same as at units in Britain except that work started at 6.30 am and finished in time for a late lunch, leaving ample spare time. At the weekend between the two visits it had become customary to fill the Dakota with instructors and their wives and fly to Livingstone, the airfield for the Victoria Falls and their famous hotel. On one occasion I had been stuck at the airfield, combing Africa for a spare Dakota tyre, one of mine having been punctured and mending being out of the question. BOAC, as it then was, offered an exchange but wanted £80 for delivery of the spare from Nairobi. Being at Livingstone for a jolly was condoned but lacking in formal authority, and I was at a loss for a story that would prevent an enquiry. Providence intervened when the Southern Rhodesian Air Force came to the rescue by flying in a tyre and jacks from Salisbury. Pouring with sweat, the crew and I made the change and saved those much appreciated *sub rosa* jollies.

The next trip, Bell-free, was in a Valetta (the RAF version of the Viking airliner). We followed the standard route but stopped, nostalgically for me, at Fayid, now a major base. We then turned right towards Khartoum and all stations south. On the night trip to Juba, out in the wilds of central Africa, I was concerned at the lack of a signal from the radio beacon there, which acted as an auditory lighthouse in featureless territory. I feared that there had been a gross navigational error. I was wrong. The navigation, done by Brian Slater, a multi-skilled pilot and examiner, was perfect, Juba turning up just as dawn broke. It emerged on landing that the beacon, housed at the foot of the control tower, had had to be abandoned in the middle of the night when a lion put its head through the window. The subsequent visits went swimmingly in both senses, with little changed except for Heany's two relief landing grounds. They tested the student pilots' perceptions as well as their navigation, being named respectively Mias and Mielbow.

A tiny contretemps afflicted me at the end of an intermissionary visit to the Falls Hotel when, having left, I had to dash back to my room to collect a forgotten briefcase. There on the bed, minutes after

I had vacated, was a huge, deep pink corset. Out of the bathroom stormed its owner, a vast South African matron of the same shade. Her thick Boer accent added venom to her imprecation as I fled. On my last trip I made up for the gaffe at a stop on the way to South Africa when the distraught pilot of a private aircraft, owned by a South African diamond magnate, told me that he had left the aircraft documents, without which civil aircraft could not move, at Bulawayo. His boss, he pleaded, would sack him if his lapse caused a delay. We flew back there and retrieved them. On the resumed southward journey we flew over the majestic but brutal Kruger Memorial, doing a visit to the flying training unit at Dunottar, where the South African Air Force pilots' flying was as awful as their hospitality was lavish.

For the journey home, against my judgement because of the possibility of terminal problems of unserviceability caused by lack of spares, we had a change of route insisted on by Russell Bell. It took us through South West Africa by way of Kasama and Kumalo to the evocatively named cities of what was still the Belgian Congo – Stanleyville and Leopoldville, each with old colonial architecture comparable with that of Bombay. We continued through what had been the White Man's Grave (the part of Africa in which many Europeans died due to malaria and other diseases), staying overnight in Lagos, drearily familiar. After pit stops at Freetown and Dakar we fetched up at another colonial outpost, this time in Spanish Equatorial Africa: Villa Cisneros, on the western coastal extremity, with wonderfully cheap rooms and good food at the state-owned parador. My fears of mechanical trouble did not materialize and we returned by way of Gibraltar, now possessed of a luxurious runway, and Bordeaux.

Rachel and the boys were enjoying plentiful company and amusements at Little Rissington. Mother hen to all was Mrs Kean, wife of the well-named chief instructor of instructors whom we examiners unkindly referred to as 'the peasants'. Such was Mrs K's zeal for good works by her chickens that career advancement for their husbands lay in the making of soft toys as Christmas presents for the airmen's families. They made so many that each child could have had a dozen for the asking. It was as well that Tom Kean was replaced by Bill Coles, a former CO of 233 Squadron and an old friend, and his wife, also a former police person.

My taste for the wide world had a final fling when I took an enlarged team to Hong Kong, out by the ordinary route by way of Saigon in pre-war Vietnam, to Pakistan and thence to Mafraq in Jordan and Rayak in the Lebanon. Hong Kong was about to have its fighter defence augmented with Vampires and I was asked to assess Sek Kong, a small relief airfield, for its suitability for jet fighters. The best available vehicle was an old Beaufighter, whose twin engines were piston-operated but powerful enough to give the Beau a performance and handling characteristics not unduly different from those of the Vampire.

I took off from Kai Tak, flew round the coast to Sek Kong and did a number of successful tight circuits and approaches within the mountain-sided valley in which it lay. Satisfied that the Vampires would have no trouble, I did one more approach and touchdown. As I climbed away an engine failed. Doing an asymmetric (single-engined) circuit within the narrow compass of the valley would have been unwise. Little better was the alternative of going straight ahead towards a gap in the mountains, the touch-and-go problem of that resort being whether its very slow rate of climb would suffice for the Beau to surmount it. I chose the latter, gaining just enough height to scrape over the gap. The relief of making it to the other side was only momentary because I was now over Communist China and liable to be jumped by fighters. I was soon back out to sea, turning towards Kai Tak and landing safely. Having kept air traffic control well informed of what was happening and why, I was relieved but not surprised that the AOC was complimentary. The Chinese accepted the Governor's apology.

On the way home we landed to refuel at Saigon and Lahore. The latter involved a long wait, for the idiotic reason that we had to clear the Pakistan customs in spite of never leaving the tarmac, let alone the airfield. Spluttering with rage when I enlisted his help, the RPAF station commander tried unsuccessfully to reason with the officials. Their stone faces reflected those of bureaucrats worldwide as we solemnly took all our bags and baggage out, carried it through the customs hall and then reloaded it.

There was no such trouble at Mafraq, or at Rayak, where we did some tests. There I was handed another problem pilot, a young cadet under threat of suspension who spoke only Arabic. He and I, in a Tiger Moth, managed well enough with signs and motions, and I was glad to have no alternative but to follow the precept of letting him get on with imitating what I did. For more than an hour he flew excellently, perhaps because of the absence of badgering, and the air attaché, Group Captain Nick Carter, whom I was to meet again at the Joint Services Staff College, was assured that my advice would be followed and his cadetship reinstated. Carter, incidentally, had done more for the Lebanese than a run-of-the-mill attaché. Most notably, he responded to a request for a slogan appropriate to the air force with: 'Nil illegitimi carborundum,' dog Latin for, 'Don't let the bastards grind you down.' I wondered what would have happened when the Lebanese found out.

Home at last, I had time to practise for a long-delayed test to raise my flying instructor's category from A2 to A1. The test could only be conducted by one of my own team of examiners, picked by lot and having it impressed on him that I was to be treated in the same way as all other candidates. He verged on the side of overzealousness, but I passed. Every candidate had to produce a personal speciality: I presented, and had accepted, night aerobatics in a Harvard, a sequence that I had put together on nights when 'the peasants' were night flying and I could be allotted a safe bit of sky, well clear of the airfield.

Added to the most welcome accolade was a surprise plus from one of the other baronial commanders-in-chief. Air Chief Marshal Sir James Robb, commander-in-chief of RAF units in Germany, which were almost an air force in themselves, had amongst his acquisitions an unarmed photo reconnaissance Spitfire, painted in the light blue camouflage and marked with his initials JMR, which he used as a personal transport. As a former commandant, he was fond of CFS and on relinquishing his command in Germany gave it to us.

By great good luck there were only two Spitfire pilots in flying practice on the station: one was the commandant, Group Captain Jarman, a pleasant New Zealander soon to be in trouble for building a boat in a hangar using RAF materials; and myself. Jarman was busy and uninterested, leaving me to look after and fly JMR, ensuring thereby that it remained serviceable. During its weekly outings I exploited its wonderful aerobatic handling qualities, which included, along with the Tiger Moth, easy eight-point hesitation rolls and good inverted flying. I had done the same from time to time in the Spitfire's naval equivalent, the Seafire, which had the minor impediment of an anal hook to enable it to be caught and brought to a halt on carrier decks.

The Navy provided other strings to my flying bow. Testing naval units meant getting into practice with their aircraft. One was the Firefly, a lumbering fighter-bomber with a wide, strengthened undercarriage to increase the success rate for carrier landings. Knowing its little ways was essential for visits to the simulated carrier deck at Henstridge, in Somerset, to check the standard of instruction in carrier landings: a very dull procedure involving endless approaches and not so much landings as almighty downward thumps.

More refreshing was the Sea Fury, the naval version of the Tempest, the last and fastest piston-engine fighter. Originally intended to destroy V-1 flying bombs, it outperformed the Vampire jet fighter. I used it at the naval air station at Lossiemouth, where there had been a dribble of fatal landing accidents affecting cadets who, having undershot the runway, applied too much power too quickly to try and get out of trouble. The sudden urge caused the huge propeller to rotate the aircraft instead of the other way round. The need, for two successive years, was for demonstrations at the runway, before an assembly of cadets, of how to 'round out' (put the aircraft in the landing posture) using safe speed and application of power.

That demonstration needed particularly thorough practice. To get it I went shortly beforehand to Lee-on-Solent to borrow a Sea Fury.

Arriving in an Anson to collect it I was agreeably surprised that the naval flight commander had kindly started the engine for me and all was ready for me to taxi away. On the next morning, back at Little Rissington, the engine (a Rolls-Royce Griffon, essentially a souped-up Merlin) would not start. After a day of prolonged and unsuccessful effort I found a flight sergeant who had serviced the RAF version of the Sea Fury, the Tempest. Clinging to the wing as I pressed the starter cartridge button with a soft-headed hammer, away went the engine. On returning the aircraft to Lee, I answered my dark blue colleague's disingenuously solicitous enquiry with, 'Oh yes, we did have a spot of trouble but nothing the RAF couldn't handle.'

Far different from that cheerful banter was an encounter after I had done the demonstration at the end of Lossie's runway during a week of testing pilots and re-categorizing naval instructors. I was shocked by the literal sea fury of the commander (Air), a choleric figure, because the RAF was doing the testing and not the senior service itself. My abiding memory of the glorious Sea Fury, however, is the sheer exhilaration of a fast run, on a glorious day, along a long stretch of the south coast on the way back to Lee. A big piston engine going flat-out has a special quality unrepeatable by a suave, silky jet.

The wing was lucky to be thrust into becoming familiar with both piston and jet trainers. Less privileged units were uncertain of how to deal with the transition and especially the 'habit patterns', as they were called, formed in flying pistons that could cause difficulty and even accidents in flying jets (a topic I wrote about later for an RAF magazine). CFS did all it could to dispel the illusion, teach flexibility and emphasize the danger of creating a self-fulfilling prophesy. The problem was aggravated by the Gloster Meteor twin-engined trainer, a thoroughly unsatisfactory aircraft and, indeed, the only aircraft I disliked. Its worst fault was its very short endurance of only forty-five minutes, reducing productive training time to about half an hour. It was unpressurised, causing a shortage of wind at one end and an indecorous excess of it at the other. It was poorly heated and uncomfortable. Cadets and some instructors were frightened of it. Its redeeming feature was a superb, easy-to-use aerobatic performance. One dashing CFS 'peasant', Flight Lieutenant Graham Hulse, used that quality on a good day for vapour trails to draw a huge phallic image in the Cotswold sky. No doubt he had the balls, temperamentally, artistically and physically, to complete the picture. But the chance never came. Before he could do so he was ordered to land and was sent away on a punitive posting on the same day.

The far superior Vampire trainer, a two-seater version of the fighter, was all that the Meteor trainer wasn't: side by side seating, a delight to fly and throw about, and pressurized to make pilots immune to fart attacks. It was so exhilarating that I overdid the antics on a practice solo trip and spinning trial. In a spin I couldn't be sure whether the aircraft was upside down or the right way up, and thus whether recovery needed forward or backward movement of the control column. In the event I fell out of the sky with such a sudden height loss that, having a cold, I punctured an eardrum. I terrified Rachel with a big patch of blood on my pillow in the middle of the following night and was grounded for four miserable weeks. The Vampire's only drawback was its awful heating system. The pilot could select either 'hot', in which case the cockpit filled with steam, or 'cold', which provided Christmassy festoons of tiny ice cubes. We cursed the makers, Sir George Godfrey and Partners, who had had the gall to put their nameplate on the cockpit control.

As the age of the piston-engined aircraft waned, I was glad not to have missed it. The Avro Anson, formerly a bomber, a twin-engined trainer pre-dating the Oxford and now a light transport, was so easy to fly that one questioned its moral character: 'Fill me up and I'm anybody's.' The de Havilland Devon, a glorified Anson and the military version of the civil Dove, similarly docile, felt like a sheet of paper to fly. The Balliol and the Provost, respective attempts to replace the timeless Harvard and the Prentice, were humdrum. The real success was the Jet Provost, used for so long as the staple RAF trainer that it became a classic.

All in all, I had a wonderful eighteen months' tour at CFS, flying over a sizeable slice of the world in a variety of aircraft of which I could hardly have dreamt, competent to test on all of them and able, almost at will, to enjoy them on my own account. Unworthily, I lusted after an Air Force Cross, which I knew had been awarded for much less. That award, however, was rationed, and for what I can only surmise was a matter of inter-service politics, the one available went to a naval lieutenant, a stalwart of 'the peasants' but remarkable only in that he wore dark and not light blue.

All I got was this lousy Queen's Commendation for Valuable Service in the Air, entitling me to the oak leaf, worn, in common with a mention in dispatches, as the last item in a row of medals. Ho hum; now for a penitential year as a staff college student.

Chapter 13

A Good Grounding

Golf and bridge I had forsworn. There remained the conventional method of moving onwards and upwards in the RAF, which was to go to the staff college and do well. Thanks to the good facilities at Cranwell for preparation, I had sailed through the qualifying exam and my turn came in 1952.

A stately home in Bracknell, its grounds enormously and hideously built on, housed the main college. The ostensible object was to train officers for higher command and staff appointments, but it also acted as a sifter of wheat from chaff. An even more important function was the indoctrination of students of the case for the continued existence of the RAF. The propaganda began during kindergarten exercises in speaking and thinking. One was a précis of an article in a 1949 *Sunday Times* headed 'Britain needs a Bomber Force'. It was so well written as to be easy to shorten and nobody, I feel sure, thought any more about it. That did not prevent the staff from distributing, eight months later, a minute assuring us that Slessor was still of that opinion and attaching a copy of an official pamphlet, also by him:

An air force of today without its long-range bomber force would be like a navy of pre-1914 days without its Line of Battle ... The British four-jet bombers are the best in their class in the world. Are we to be content to provide as our Pax Atlantica the ground support and maritime aircraft to defend ourselves? ... If we did, we should have little or no influence ... In peace, we should lose what influence we have on American policy ...

This was nationalist spin, very different from his well reasoned article arguing that the bomber has a place in the balanced air force essential to national defence.

The whole pamphlet, a world away from the article, was as pure a piece of propaganda as the leaflets I dropped on many raids, oxymoronically combining nationalist bombast and sycophancy of America. It reinforced the unease I felt about other bits of the course. Meanwhile, it was amusing to draw on my Selection Board experience to reciprocate the obvious assessment process applied to the students by the grandly named Directing Staff.

Boredom waned when we moved on to the formal appreciations, which were the military modality for channelling and disciplining thought. In an elementary setting we learnt to select an aim; state how we reached it; list a multiplicity of factors such as time and space, own and enemy forces and weather; weigh the significance of each in relation to the others and the whole; forecast what would happen; and conclude with what to do and a plan for doing it. The easy one was settling the hash of a minor oriental potentate called the Fakir of Ipi, the last of the unruly tribes dealt with entirely by the RAF in 1938; grist, perhaps, to the indoctrination mill. The difficult task was Exercise See Adler (Sea Lion), which involved planning the German invasion of Britain in 1940. Most students found them instructive and amusing but a few became overwrought. Applying pressure was part of the sifting process and there were rumours of past breakdowns and even suicides, the latter at the bigger and tougher Army Staff College at Camberley. I saw nothing of that except the anxiety of a friend, a very bright engineer, who spent nights walking about and worrying. Incidentally, my half-brother, William, was on the directing staff (DS) at Camberley.

The DS, often being cruel to be kind, were a mixed bunch. At the top was the intelligent and perceptive Air Vice-Marshal Peter Gilmore, for whom, when he became deputy head of the Far East

Air Force, I gained great respect. Below him were a stolid air commodore and four group captains. One was an over-promoted golfer; all pipe smoke and odoriferous tweeds. At the opposite end was Bernard Chacskfield, one of a very select few who, having started as a boy entrant ascended effortlessly through the ranks. Tall, diffident and approachable, he was the best of the whole faculty, eventually becoming an air vice-marshal. Of the wing commander workers, mostly bright, the most interesting was Christopher Foxley-Norris, a prominent battle of Britain pilot reputed to be legally qualified but, as I discovered years later, had only done the bit of training as a barrister.

There was much socializing, part of the assessment process. I had never been much of a socialiser. I was habitually untidy, deficient in small talk and good at getting stranded at cocktail parties. School fees being what they were becoming, I tried to make clothes last and was never quite as well turned out as I should have been, commuting on the Royal Enfield 150cc motorbike doing me no sartorial favours. Rachel made up for me, but we shared a dislike for entertainment that was so obviously used as a vehicle for the gain or loss of points.

We were lucky to get relief from non-college contacts. We had found a spacious flat in a big house in Camberley, with wooded grounds sloping down to the main road to London and opposite the landmark Blue Pool – large, clean and much enjoyed by the boys. One of the other two flats housed the owners, a quiet, mouldering couple whose hobby was drinking. In the third flat, above us, booze was a way of life and potential death. The tenant, a doctor, burly and bloated, took his resident girlfriend out every night in their tattered Rolls, both returning drunk and spending the small hours in noisy brawls. On one sad occasion the teenage son of one of them came to stay, knocking us up in the middle of a particularly noisy night and asking for a bed, which, of course, we provided. I ought to have done something about the doctor's drink-driving. I did not; I can only plead overwork and the subject's lack of salience at the time.

Happily, we were close to William, his wife Barbara, and their family of four. He could certainly have slipped me copies of the 'pinks', which were the staff solutions to set problems, so named because they were printed on paper of that colour. Neither of us would have done that; but he did pass on what he could find out about how I was doing. The answer, I blush to say, was very well.

Another pressure that manifested itself as the weeks passed was having several tasks on the go simultaneously: long, drawn-out exercises, essays and practice speeches being piled up on top of each other. That was a feature of lasting value, as was the deliberate racking of nerves in drafting and making speeches. When my turn came to address the whole community for five minutes I had already sat through enough orations to observe that light and funny topics did much better than solemn ones. Having in mind a lampoon of the staff for which the college magazine editor had asked, I presented it in embryo, ending with a suggestion about how to deal with our mentors in the mock Latin tag I had heard from Nick Carter. To my amazed delight it got the biggest laugh of the course so far, as well as that of my still very slight public speaking career. I owed a good deal to the scene shifter, stage manager and general factotum for the college hall, an old stager in two senses, called Irish. Moments before I began, he had eased my tremor by whispering, 'Remember, Sir, every good artist must have temperament.'

There was soon more bomber indoctrination. We had to do a close study of an analysis of the results of RAF bombing in Germany, set out in individually loaned copies of a book as big as *The Times Atlas* and not much thinner, classified as confidential. Having signed the Official Secrets Act, I forbear to give away what it contained, but it brought home to me how very little all the early effort and sacrifice that characterized the Wellington operations in the Middle East had achieved. It made light of the fact that it was only in and after 1942, when Pathfinder (guide aircraft dropping coloured flares for the main force to aim at) operations began in earnest that the bomber offensive against Germany had begun to bite. I cannot remember reading anything about the real effect on civilian morale in Germany, which was to bolster rather than damage it, as in Britain. Nor did the study make clear that it was the USAF daylight raids (of which 178 Squadron, myself included, had played an arduous part in trying out) and their destruction of oil resources that had triggered the German surrender. Nothing in the tome, I felt sure, was factually wrong. It was simply that the work was more one of advocacy than of analysis.

Not the least benefit of the course was mixing with the students – RAF, soldier, sailor and American – in a comradeship of benevolent adversity. We were kept together by the senior student, Wing Commander the Honourable Hugh Dowding, bearing that epithet because his father was Lord Dowding, Marshal of the RAF and Commander-in-Chief of Fighter Command when it won the Battle of Britain. It was Dowding, on the editorial committee, who had asked me for a lampoon. I offered half a page of rhyming couplets headed with my laugh-getting gag. Too long and in-jokey to quote in full, it included:

Can they [the staff] *simply subside into posts designed for ordinary mortals?*
Or should they be raised at once to the heights reserved for [former Chiefs of staff] *Trenchards, Tedders and Portals?*
Surely they should rise to the top, and there settle every major issue with sublime economy of nisu [effort, lifted from the College motto; also a quotation from one of the canonical Principles of War]
Should there not be a special new directorate designed specifically to sort out and expectorate the top chaff,
and replace it with members of the Directing Staff?
... Can it be
That high-ups sometime think the same as we
and wonder
whether there wouldn't be an occasional high-powered blunder
if these, our mentors, were to see the day come
when they were bereft of their roseate vade mecum?

I was pleased to have that offering accepted because with it in the same issue went a ponderous article of mine about pilot problems in the jet age, which ended:

there is a danger inherent in the nature of an armed service that new technical developments may outstrip the progress in training and organization which must accompany them ... The race to deploy supersonic aircraft ... is too fast and too closely contested to allow these habits to play their traditional part in the jet age ... We can avoid trammelling the men we have with a training system out of tune with the times ... Only by doing so can we avoid the penalty of failing to produce the men to match the hour.

This we did. RAF flying training was adapted and refined. It became, and remains, an exemplar to the rest of the world.

Getting two items printed was highly unusual. There would, the tweedy group captain explained, have been a third if it hadn't been for the other two. The subject was nationalism in British Africa, set by the college and accompanied by a long list of references that I ferreted out and read. It has not survived. Just as well.

There were occasional escapes from the grind of studying. One outlet was educative visits. Mine included the Bristol Aeroplane Company at Filton Airfield, where the mighty Brabazon prototype was taking shape. It was as fascinating from a technical standpoint as was its naming after Lord Brabazon of Tara, a giant pioneering pilot whose licence number, issued at the turn of the twentieth century, was 'One'. The Brab, as it was called, was the forbear of the Britannia, for many years a mainstay of British civil and military transport.

A contrasting visit was to a submarine base, where my under-water trip convinced me that I had chosen the better of the fluid media. There was also a tour of *The Times*, taking in the panelled majesty of the leader writers' room. I could not imagine that I would later have upwards of fifty letters printed in its august pages, almost always expressing dissent.

The best escapes were my more or less weekly outings to White Waltham Airfield, near Reading, where there were Anson, Proctor, Chipmunk Prentice and Spitfire aircraft as well as a T21 glider, in which staff and students could keep in practice. They were all a delight to fly – particularly the Anson, mainstay of many communication flights and general dogsbody ever since its debut in 1936. I had re-qualified as Command Instrument Examiner (CIRE) – a new and even grander feather in my flying helmet – just before leaving CFS and so could renew the ratings of the keen and competent.

I also scored points for brushing up the aerobatics of one of the wing commander staffers. I and another CIRE, a fellow student, Squadron Leader Leonard Cherry, head of the CFS subordinate testing outfit in Home Command, were able, incestuously but legitimately, to renew each other at the end of the course. That was to come in useful in the Far East. I marvel at the conscientious way in which we tested each other. Tragically, he killed himself accidentally a year or two later doing a demonstration landing for the pilots of his squadron in Germany, similar to the ones I had done at Lossiemouth.

A sour contrast to the other flying was a trip in a glider with a US Navy lieutenant commander who, he assured me, had ample gliding experience and needed only to be familiarized with the T21. He was so self-assured that I failed to intervene in his poorly judged approach and he landed us short of the airfield in a field of growing corn. With a squad of helpers we humped the undamaged craft 200 yards back to the airfield. As constant reminders ensured, I was not allowed to forget an incident in an otherwise unblemished gliding career.

At the end of the course I was posted to the Far East Air Force (FEAF). A friend and co-student, Derek Thirlwell, was also going, getting the influential job of personal staff to the Commander-in-Chief. He was to go by troopship with his wife Jill and their new baby, especially cherished because he had long been tried for. To the proud parents' pleasure, I observed that somebody else would have to be prime minister while he was swimming the Channel. I, as I smugly boasted to anyone who would listen (not many), was needed so urgently for a vital new post in Intelligence that I was having to go at once by air.

Chapter 14

An Airman Abroad

I left Rachel and the boys in Glastonbury, where fortunately there was an adequate school near her parents' house. They were to follow by troopship when their turn came. I spent a day in London being briefed by assorted military and civil authorities listed on a slip of paper marked 'Secret', which, to my horror, I lost. Nobody handed it in and thus I escaped some condign penalty. From the briefings it emerged that I was to be the RAF staff officer at FEAF, based at Changi, responsible for the RAF intelligence contribution to the Five Power Staff Agency, the embryo of a Far Eastern version of NATO named SEATO and comprising Britain, the US and France (the last still with a presence in Indo-China).

I flew as a passenger in a Hastings, the standard RAF transport that, having been in service since 1948, was the oldest aircraft still in use. We were on a new, speeded-up schedule with slipping crews. The journey took thirty-two all-but-continuous flying hours. Arriving at Changi, the main base of the three RAF airfields on Singapore Island, late at night, I was met by Wing Commander Bill Arney, Deputy Head of Intelligence at FEAF. He was welcoming but mildly surprised at the urgency with which I had been flown out. Next morning I found out why. The Five Power Staff Agency had yet to exist. When it did, it would generate no work for months at least, and even then there would be enough capacity to deal with it within the more than ample intelligence. As for SEATO, such were the disputes among the candidate nations, that years could well pass before it existed. It took Isaiah 63:5 to express my response:

And I looked and there was none to help; and I wondered that there was none to uphold; therefore my own arm brought salvation unto me; and my fury it upheld me.

As I unravelled what had happened, the zephyr of my discontent with the RAF became a breeze. The chief intelligence officer at FEAF was an old, long passed-over group captain. In his bitterness he consoled himself by waging the turf wars that were always fought in large headquarters. The very name Five Power Staff Agency had enough buzz for him to put in for another staff officer; and he argued successfully that Intelligence rather than Planning should be the place to put him. The opposing case went by default because the admirable chief of Planning, Group Captain Whiteley, saw through what was happening and would have none of it. The Establishments Committee, whose job it was to curb demands for extra staff, had been hoaxed, if not hexed. I was the victim. I used my own arm to bring salvation by looking for something to do. Bill Arney could not help. He was gentle, good-natured and no match for our appalling boss. He was a pre-war Cranwell product of very modest achievement and my impression was that he had simply given up. One of the other squadron leaders told me, not entirely frivolously, what he did in Bill's department: arriving in the office each morning, he adjusted the date-to-view wall calendar, and having noted the new date, he turned the page in his diary. That was it.

True to Isaiah and remembering the dictum of Jeeves' aunt, which he used as advice to Bertie Wooster, that there is always a way, I found one. Another squadron leader, Philip Gee, had just arrived with his family to become the RAF member of the Joint Intelligence Staff (JIS) Far East, based at Phoenix Park, on the far side of Singapore – a formidable commute. Gee cared far less about what he did, and had just found a house near Changi. Unlike me, he was unconcerned at the prospect of two-and-a-half years in a non-job, so, together, we asked for a swap and got it. I relished the prospect of having something that sounded interesting to do.

The JIS offered exactly that. I worked with a naval lieutenant commander, Pat Dane; a gunner soldier, Peter White, and a Foreign Office principal, Robert John. Phoenix Park was the headquarters of the Commissioner General for South East Asia; at the time, Malcolm Macdonald, a former Labour MP of great charm and diplomatic nous. The JIS wrote papers for and briefed the Joint Intelligence Committee (JIC) Far East, servicing its weekly meetings. The JIC's main job was to keep watch on the Far East to see who was giving cause for warning the Foreign Office and the local embassies and garrisons. The joint structure replicated on a small scale the JIC and the Chiefs of Staff Committee in London, where the two were linked by the Defence and Overseas Policy Committee, aptly named DOPO. We tried to be particularly vigilant about armaments, oil and a scarcely less important resource – rice. Shortages and even significant changes in sources and supplies could cause riots, revolutions and even wars.

One of our regular surveys came last on a wearisome agenda of a meeting of the top body, the British Defence Co-ordinating Committee, chaired by Malcolm Macdonald. Asked by the Secretary how he wanted the rice paper dealt with, he replied, 'Oh, stick it on the bottom of macaroons.'

Much of our other work included studies for the Joint Planning Staff of what to go for in various contingencies. One was the seizure of a beach head on the Chinese mainland, recommending such suitable entry points as the ports of Amoy and Foochow should so hazardous a venture become expedient. Another was a major commercial study of a possible Communist plan for the invasion of South East Asia, anticipating the name of an invalid food with the code name Complan. There was a varied diet of actuality: the Communist threat in Malaya and its suspected supporters amongst venal politicians in Singapore, the Hukbalahap rebels in the Philippines, sounding as if they were part of a Doolittle voyage; the rumbling hostility at a flashpoint where Communist artillery habitually fired on the Nationalist Quemoy and Matsu islands. A spectator sport to be watched through secret sources was the mainland government's clumsy campaign to subvert the Chiang Kai-shek (known rather rudely as Chancre Jack) Nationalists in Taiwan. The worst worry was the steady erosion of French control of Indo-China manifest in their habitual taking of short-term soft options and their chronic state of denial about the approaching defeat by Viet Cong revolutionaries at Dien Bien Phu. Their conduct emulated the incompetence and corruption that did for France herself in 1940. All of this I found fascinating.

For three months I lived in the most beautiful mess in the RAF. Fairy Point, on the eastern tip of Singapore Island, was a large colonial-style building overlooking the bosky Malayan coast across an idyllic stretch of water. We were near Hell on the Hill, the nickname of the enormous FEAF headquarters. A mile away was Changi airfield, with the notorious Changi Gaol nearby. British prisoners of war built the airfield under Japanese lashes and I still regret that they have no memorial for their superb construction job, terribly costly in lives. Also nearby is Changi village, a miniature version of the Singapore City shopping area featuring tailors who would run up made-to-measure tropical suits and uniform over-night. Near the surrounding RAF housing was the much-admired all-ages RAF school, from which our boys were soon to benefit.

I was invited occasionally to the conventional social event, descended from colonial days, of curry tiffin, or Sunday lunch. A dozen or so guests would have cold beer followed by Nasi goreng, easily remembered for its Nazi connotation. It was a small mound of compacted sago drizzled, as the telly cooks say, with diluted syrup. The Arneys asked me to what I thought would be such an event. I was surprised that the only other guest was a youngish, nubile airwoman. Much of the talk was smutty gossip. She was over-familiar and I inferred that her presence was my hosts' act of kindly-meant indulgence of a sexually-starved grass widower. I fear I disappointed the company by leaving as soon civility allowed.

My working life was full except at weekends. In the week I left for Phoenix Park early in the morning, getting back in time for a game of squash before dinner. Afterwards I read or did a turn of duty at the Officers' Club as a classical music disc jockey, culling culture from the back of the LP jackets. On Sunday mornings, still qualified to fly the Valetta transport, I did simulated bombing runs over Singapore City, after the fashion of those I had once done over Cairo, acting as the target for the practice interceptions by the fighters and controllers of the Singapore Auxiliary Air Force. Still entitled to do instrument rating tests, I helped to keep my fellow staff officers and the crews of the Far East Communication Squadron up to date. There were also suspicious-looking ships in the Singapore Harbour roads to be photographed at mast height from the Harvard, which I also used for aerobatic practice in skies much less restricted than at home. Derek Thirlwell settled into his tied house and, constantly hospitable, enjoyed my CFS party piece of night aerobatics as a passenger in a Harvard's front cockpit, doubtless recounting the experience to his popular and well-respected boss, Air Marshal Sir Clifford Sanderson, and other worthies: more points scored, I hoped.

Life improved enormously with the arrival of Rachel and the boys in the troopship *Dilwara*, known for its rolling. We put up in the Grand Hotel, a glorified boarding house and a rite of passage for new arrivals until they found proper housing. David, playing in the grounds, was seen by an *amah* (nanny) employed by the Lee family next door and was invited to play with their child in their enormous garden. In the best intelligence tradition I checked up on the family. As was apparent from a pillar of brass plates on the wall of a giant office block in the city, the Lees had interests in rubber, real estate, shipping, oil, wharfage and just about every other major undertaking on the island. We needn't have worried.

We soon found a house on the main Singapore-Changi road. Drawing on the very generous allowances for RAF families I bought a second-hand Ford Prefect for commuting, as well as other hitherto unaffordable delights, including bicycles for the boys. Both boys flourished at Changi School. I was glad to observe in Gregor the dawn of logical thinking. Lounging on our bed as I dressed for a dinner at Changi, he had to be told not to fiddle with the bedside light. Grown-ups, I explained, could get nasty shocks from touching lights; and if children, being smaller, did it, they could be badly hurt. After a thoughtful silence, a small voice hazarded: 'And if babies did it, they'd explode.'

We toured the island in the Prefect, venturing occasionally across the Johor Causeway into the mainland of Malaysia. A lot of fun was had in such exotic places as the Haw Par Villa (a replica of a mandarin's mansion), a zoo and very good public parks. There was also St Andrew's Cathedral on Sunday mornings and every day at the Swimming Club, which could only be joined after a liturgy of meeting the assembled committee – an inspection, I later realized, was to ensure that the candidates were white. Of the marvellous shops the most remarkable was Tangs, selling Chinese wares of all kinds.

We had known all along that living in Singapore could not last long. David had already been to four schools and we knew how bad discontinuity was for education. The only solution was private education for both boys, meaning that Rachel would have to take them home for a timely start. David, unusually, was upset during their sad embarkation on what proved to be the grubby trooper *Asturias*, knowing that we were facing another year or more of separation.

I had sold the car and handed it over on the way back to Changi. Back in Fairy Point, with my RAF commuting car restored, I continued to enjoy the JIS. To save money I gave up cigarette smoking, finding no great difficulty after an unpleasant initial forty-eight hours.

My role in Sunday morning flying had changed from simulated bomber to real fighter, vectored endlessly in a Vampire towards a Valetta flown by a colleague, for the benefit of trainee controllers. (The Valetta, incidentally, was normally a load carrier developed from the civil airlines' Viking and old enough to be an exhibit in the aircraft museum at RAF Colerne.)

The turf warrior chief of FEAF Intelligence had departed. His successor was Group Captain John Roe, kind, sensible and soon to become a force in the Joint Intelligence Committee, which comprised all the service chiefs, the secret departments MI5 and MI6 representatives and, as chairman, the flamboyant Scot, Andrew

Gilchrist. Roe's success, I flattered myself, came partly from the insider's scandal-filled briefing I gave him before each meeting. I thought him high-handed for refusing, on my behalf and without consulting me, the offer of promotion to acting wing commander and a posting to another ground job at the RAF Malayan head-quarters in Kuala Lumpur. (That city had a familial link, having a Cavendish Road named after my generous uncle Alex Cavendish, who had served there as a colonial servant.)

I came round to being glad he had prevented me from embarking on what would have meant a two-year-plus separation. Promotion, he said, would soon come along anyway. It did. Meanwhile, I was happy for my old friend Dick Wakeford to get the job. Our families had been close since we both commanded flights at Cranwell, and I had done what I could a year before to help with the many problems they faced after his sister-in-law, a BOAC stewardess, had been killed in a Constellation crash at Kallang civil airport, a few miles from Changi.

The Arneys were replaced by George Badcoe, a welcome addition to the handful of Fairy Point residents and a squash opponent of exacting parity for me. Another arrival was Christopher Foxley-Norris, formerly of the Staff College, to be a wing commander planner in FEAF headquarters.

Like CFS, the JIS offered overseas intermissions to relieve monotony. We had produced a study of Indonesia's prospects and likely effects on British interests so awful that the ambassador in Jakarta suggested that we should visit the country and see for our-selves. Claiming my turn for a perk that was granted to the regular pilots of the FEAF communication flight, I borrowed the de Havilland Devon and, with the JIC Squadron secretary, Howard Lewis, a navigator, flew our three colleagues to Jakarta for a weekend. We arrived just in time for a formal luncheon for about thirty guests in the large embassy dining room. After a no-alternative slug of gin and lime we sat down, on a boiling day, to soup, roast lamb and steamed pudding, no doubt to impress the guests with what British-ness really meant. We then went for a hilarious two-night stay in the embassy's holiday cottage in the hills, set in a tea plantation and comparable to a miniature version of the hill stations of the Indian Raj. After talks with the head of Chancery – a sort of diplomatic major domo – and with secretaries graded first, second and third, I flew the party, hung-over, but wiser, back to Changi.

Much sooner than expected, the Five Power Staff Agency came into being. The JIS, it was decided, were readymade junior British representatives, doing the unfortunate Philip Gee, whose job it should have been, out of his appointed task. For the connoisseur of trips abroad, as I now was, this one could hardly have been more idyllic. It was to Hawaii, where we went in a US Military Transport Service (MATS) DC4, virtually an enlarged Dakota. The route took us to Guam, a magic Pacific island of surf and sea birds marred only by the paraphernalia of USAF aeroplanes. On Oahu, the main Hawaiian island, we worked on joint contingencies, which, had they materialized, would have provoked nuclear war. We were much hampered by French intransigence and the constant referral of trivial decisions to Paris. We worked only from 7.00 am until 1.00 pm, usually spending the afternoons on Waikiki Beach, a large slice of which had been appropriated by the US Army for its own use. One amusement was to walk to the adjoining bit of public beach, where elderly American tycoons were to be seen consorting and often cavorting with young ladies they had brought and were accommodating at the Royal Hawaiian Hotel, which backed onto the sands. Another diversion was a tour of Pearl Harbor, where the cadavers of the battleships bombed on 7 December 1941 have been left as they lay – eerily similar, in retrospect, to the gaunt beauty of the ruins of Dresden, also left as memorials to acts of infamy, which I visited years later as a general for peace.

The US services gave the delegations a formal cocktail party hosted by the commander of the Pacific Fleet (CINCPAC), at the time, Admiral Felix B. Stump. He was an archetypal war lord of the General MacArthur stamp. We were each presented to him almost as if to royalty. If, during conversation, a query or an item he thought worth remembering came up, he would snap his fingers at one of the white-uniformed ensigns standing stock still in the corners of the room, who would hasten to the master, notebook at the ready, do his bidding and then hasten back to their station. The only lightening of the Teutonic rigidity I saw was traffic slow-downers on the domestic housing access roads labelled 'Stump's Bumps'.

The civilians were different. At her cocktail party for the visiting military, a leathery hostess expressed her interest in the love life of the queen's sister, Princess Margaret, who had fallen for an air equerry, Group Captain Peter Townsend, and then, under pressure from the Palace and the Archbishop of Canterbury, thrown him over. She had also read about Hewlett Johnson, Dean of Canterbury, notorious for his communist leanings and known as the Red Dean. She conflated the two in her question to me: 'How come the Red Dean won't let that koin'l [colonel] marry your queen?' the unravelling of which taxed my interpretative abilities.

My last overseas outing took place across the South China Sea in the Philippines, now a member of the shadowy South East Asia Treaty Organisation, which in the event was to come to nothing. After a reception in the presidential palace in the grubby city of Manila and a handshake from the jolly old King Coal President Magsaysay, we went to work in the town of Baguio (a hill resort that had never taken off) in the Pines Hotel, beautifully situated in forest surroundings. I shared a room with a gentle old Carthusian contemporary whom I had known only slightly. He was more interested in antique silver than his career, which was soon to end. The soldier, Peter White, was highly thought of in Singapore and deserved a better career than he had had: at the end of it he went into property in southern Spain. The three of us worked on another series of abstruse contingency plans.

In our spare time we climbed the beautiful Mount Santo Tomas. The marvellous view of the islands reminded me of a bit of Isaac Watts' hymn *There is a Land of Pure Delight* (AMR 545):

> *Could we but climb where Moses stood,*
> *and view the landscape o'er.*

I wondered for a long time what the 'landscibor' was.

There was much social activity between the five nations, consisting mostly of very trying cocktail parties. I was saddled with hosting and escorting two Thai generals, that rank being considered appropriate to the work done for which the other allies used majors. They were charming, medal-bedecked little men with little English and unpronounceable names. They were paroxysmal with laughter whenever, with their delighted permission, I introduced them at functions using as their names two airfields in Thailand that I could remember and pronounce. I found the recollection easy because, had they only known, the airfields (Prachuap Kirikan and Nakhon Si Thammarat) had been under surveillance.

We returned to Singapore to find that our diplomat colleague Robert John had been promoted and posted to Saigon, where he and his wife Ann went to great trouble to find their small son a kindergarten, eventually coming across a hugely expensive French establishment. Their reward became clear when the child came home after the first morning and, asked what he had learnt, his delighted reply was: 'fighting, spitting and wee-wees in the garden.'

Robert's successor was the incandescently bright Meriel Russell. She improved the quality of our work, which had earned us a complimentary letter from Malcolm Macdonald, who was leaving to become High Commissioner in India:

> a constant series of weighty matters receiving ... always the most thorough ... expert advice ... working long and late ... tireless and able assistance ... Personally and officially I am deeply indebted.

It was OTT but welcome all the same.

Hoping that my 'bachelor' life might be ended prematurely, I applied for a course at the RAF Flying College at Manby in Lincolnshire, where Wing Commander Russell Bell, under whose command I had writhed at the Central Flying School, had been on the staff. I was delighted to be accepted, thereby getting home in February 1956 instead of July. The course would almost certainly get

The hated kilt.

'Be Prepared' is the Scout motto.
At the Jamboree.

The wreath-laying achieved with great relief. (*Illustrated London News*)

Back from a raid, trying at nineteen to look macho.

Portraits of the author and the family crest – deceased ravens ensconced.

Balmanno, near Montrose, the family home that was lost.

Andy's desert crash, so near and yet so far from the airfield.

Supply dropping at Arnhem, October 1944, Flight Lieutenant David Lord earning the VC.

The glider that landed in a corn field.

... suspicious looking ships in the Singapore harbour roads, Chinese Communist victims of the author's airborne camera.

Advice from friend and colleague Major Peter White, no doubt about a weighty matter.

The Sirdana of Sokoto getting a quote for a Vulcan.

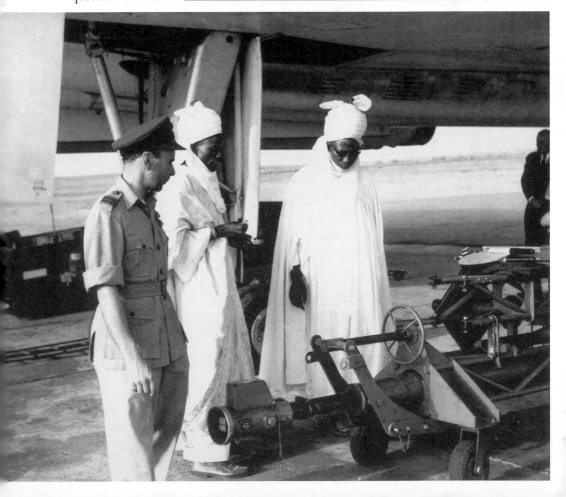

An exhilarated crew arriving in Ceylon en route for the Far East.

Keeping busy while the Hastings was grounded. The author's two sons enjoyed a dual in the Chipmunk.

Jnctuous joke in return for a compliment from a senior officer.

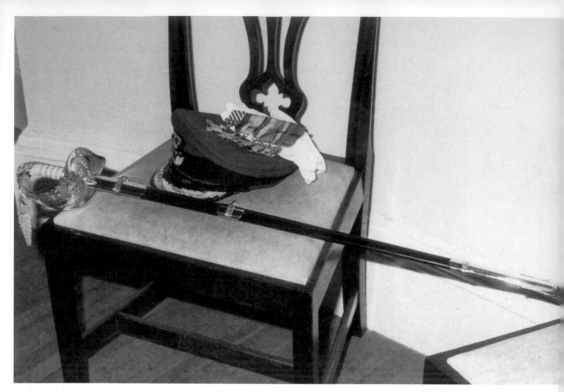

The Esso sword and other clobber in the mayor's parlour at Bath.
(Crown copyright)

NO 3
PUMP COURT
Third Floor
Mr & Mrs A.C.L.MACKIE
Second Floor
Mr & Mrs J.E. SCATCHERD
First Floor
Mr B.W.BUDD
Mr R.C. TERRY
Mr A. LUNZER

The barristers' version of a brass plate.

THIS TABLET WAS ERECTED BY THE BRITISH 61st DIVISION TO COMMEMORATE FALLEN COMRADES

THE DIVISION FIRST SERVED DURING THE GREAT WAR IN THE NEIGHBOURHOOD OF THIS TOWN OF LAVENTIE AND IS PROUD TO LEAVE ITS DEAD SLEEPING IN THE SACRED SOIL OF FRANCE

LA 61EME DIVISION BRITANNIQUE A SES CAMARADES TOMBES AU CHAMP D'HONNEUR

CETTE DIVISION QUI ENGAGEA SES PREMIERS COMBATS AU COURS DE LA GUERRE 1914 1918, DANS LE VOISINAGE DE LAVENTIE EST FIERE DE LAISSER REPOSER SES MORTS DANS LA TERRE SACREE DE FRANCE

The 61st Division memorial at Laventie, Pas-de-Calai.

The Hall at Edzell, still a white elephant today.

Both together at investiture.

Middle Temple Hall transformed by new lights presented by Sir Jules Thorn (Honorable Society of the Middle Temple).

الى كل عربى كريم

السلام عليكم ورحمة الله وبركاته وبعد فحامـــل هـذا الكتاب ضابط بالجيش
البريطانى وهو صديق وفى لكافة الشعوب العربية فنرجو أن تعـاملونه بالعطف والاكـرام .
وأن تحافظوا على حياته من كل طارى. ونأمل عند الاضطرار أن تقـدموا له ما يحتاج
اليه من طعام وشراب .

وأن ترشـدونه الى أقرب معسكر بريطانى

وسنكافئكم ماليا بسخاء على ما تسدونه اليه من خدمات .

والسـلام عليكم ورحمة الله وبركاته ؟

القيادة البريطانية العامة فى الشرق

To All Arab Peoples - Greetings and Peace be upon you. The bearer of
this letter is an Officer of the English Government and a friend of all Arabs.
Treat him well, guard him from harm, give him food and drink, help him
to return to the nearest English soldiers and you will be rewarded. Peace
and the Mercy of God upon you.

The British High Command in the East.

Useful Words

English	Arabic	English	Arabic
English	Ingleezi.		
English Flying Officer	Za-bit Ingleezi Tye-yar.	Water	Moya.
Friend	Sa-hib, Sa-deek.	Food	A'-kl.

Take me to the English and you will be rewarded.
Hud-nee eind el Ingleez wa ta-hud mu-ka-fa.

PME/1554-9/41

A so-called goolie chit for aircrew shot down, to give to capturing Senussi tribesmen.

Arthur Read, station officer and talented portraitist at work.

Locals of the Nile Delta.

Alastair Mackie, 2012.

me back into full-time flying instead of the job on the side it had been in Singapore. It was also a good career move; but that seemed to matter less and less.

Flown home by Airwork in the civil version of the Hastings, I was glad to meet an old master pilot (the highest non-commissioned flying rank) whom I had known at CFS. He had retired to the double job of first officer with Airwork and beekeeper at home. He made me welcome on the flight deck. I had the job of OC troops, consisting of nothing more than keeping an eye on the time-expired service people and their families who, as I had been told they always did, behaved impeccably. My one service to them took place on a freezing February night when we fetched up in an almost deserted customs hall at Heathrow. Just as a horde of customs men were descending on us, I saw a group of people with winter sports equipment passing through almost untouched. Running across to the head customs officer, I pleaded for my charges, just home, I said, from years on the frontiers of civilization serving queen and country, and much more deserving of leniency than the tourists, fresh from the sybaritic snowfields. He at once shifted the whole pack from us to them.

Chapter 15

White Giants on Parade

During my disembarkation leave we moved from Glastonbury, where the boys had gone back to the Tor School, which they had left a year or so earlier. Our new abode was a charming bungaloid cottage at Saltfleetby, near Louth, and within bicycle range of the good permanent station at RAF Manby. At last David could start a continuum of schooling at Ardingly College in Sussex, chosen largely because of the new reformist head, George Snow. Our younger boy, Gregor, went to the wonderfully good, single-teacher village school opposite the cottage.

We were in an idyllic setting beside a brook, but the cottage had a feature adverse even to us, experienced in abodes of variable quality as we were. The lavatory, in a converted outhouse beside the cottage proper, had a cistern fed by rainwater from the sloping roof: efficient and economical in rainy weather, but disruptive of good sanitary routine when it was dry.

A car, for the time being, was beyond our means, but I bought a second-hand bicycle for commuting. It served well except after a boozy dinner, when, in full mess kit, it catapulted me into a drainage ditch. It renewed my youthful pleasure in cycling (which has continued ever since), conveying me on Sundays to the churches of Saltfleetby All Saints and its sister, St Peter, both equipped with simple American organs. 'I was glad', as one of my favourite anthems puts it, to help out. But the extent of my amateurishness was apparent on the Sunday when one of the hymns was *Ye Holy Angels Bright*. Fulfilling the exhortation in the first verse to 'assist our song' ordinarily meant playing in B flat, which imports four black notes. Doubting my ability to remember them, I transposed the tune upwards to middle C, free from the dark invaders. All very well for me; but when we got to: 'or else the theme too high doth seem,' that was just what happened.

Soon we all had bikes and went for expeditions to the small resort of Mablethorpe on the nearby coast. A railway line from there to Louth, with a village stop, added interest to our lives. It was a great help when Gregor had a prolonged stay in Louth Cottage Hospital with another bout of a mysterious illness that had afflicted him in Singapore. It eventually turned out to be rheumatic fever, later preventing him from fulfilling his intense desire to follow me into the RAF.

Work at Manby began with a short refresher course, which I welcomed because, being already in good flying practice, I could fly for fun. I brushed up my aerobatics in a Meteor IV, a solo version faster and with a longer duration than the Mark VII, at the scruffy wartime airfield used as a satellite for Manby – Strubby. It was an evocative name, which I tried to propagate as an epithet for poor flying ('that was a strubby approach you just did') but I doubt whether it took hold. I was able to repay the flight commander's indulgence when a posse of very senior officers paid an inspection visit. I was deputed to act as exemplar of the high standard achieved by the refresher students by, as that cheerfully disrespectful young man put it, 'making with the circuits.' In a Meteor that meant a succession of approaches, touchdowns and take-offs, known as rollers. By the time the great men showed up late, I was down to my engine's last gasps of fuel, just getting by and earning whispered thanks.

The commandant was the dapper Air Commodore Paddy Dunn, who presided over a wide-ranging course designed to broaden the experience of senior officers and acquaint them with the expanding scope and complexity of RAF flying. We students already had good backgrounds as aviators and were expected to move on to senior posts. Dunn was a perfectionist who, because of my record of high assessments in bomber, transport and instructional businesses, seemed to ask more of me than he did the other students. That he did not get, at least at first. I at once took to the smooth handling characteristics of the Canberra jet bomber, reminiscent of the Mosquito but much faster. Its snag was the multiplicity of safety features, not so much bells and whistles as switches, warning lights – 'tits', as they were affectionately termed – and emergency procedures, all of which I, and others, found hard to master. Compared with some fellow students I knew little of the fighter role, but that was providentially offset by beginner's luck: on an air firing exercise in a Meteor IV, I scored twenty hits on a target at which I had fired only ninety-nine rounds.

A bout of anxiety, which had not troubled me since I had overdone it on bomber operations, came back and added to my difficulties. Fortunately it eased as the course progressed. I had as a solid companion Bert Slade, my contemporary as a CFS examiner. Together we did navigation exercises as captain and navigator. One was a day trip in a Canberra to Malta and back; the island's powerful beacon, as of old, was a great help to two pilots used for much of their careers to the luxury of professional navigators. We all did passenger flights in the Lincoln, last in the line of heavy piston-engined bombers, to experience using the ever more complicated radar navigation and bombing devices.

Best of all for me was a brief acquaintance with the Hawker Hunter, the better of the two competitors for the new RAF standard fighter, the other being the Supermarine Swift, which barely saw the light of day. On the second of two Hunter airings I shed my kid-gloved handling of the flighty creature and went supersonic, eastwards out into the North Sea. The bang from the cockpit sit point seemed undramatic to me, but not, apparently, to the wider world. I had forgotten to report it and the local radio that evening mentioned an apparent explosion out to sea, which the lifeboat from Strumble Head on the coast of Pembrokeshire had investigated without result. It seemed best not to bang on about it.

The course ended in December 1956. I got only a chilly 'qualified' assessment, the old categories apparently being used for courses. The compensation was a posting I could hardly have dreamt of. I was to command the second squadron of Vulcan bombers, to be formed shortly. The Vulcan was already recognized as the best of the three competing types commissioned for the new generation of aircraft capable of carrying nuclear weapons. The first was the Vickers Valiant, a workhorse whose limited performance was considered inadequate to give a fair chance of surviving the expected Soviet opposition. Then there was the Vulcan, immensely sturdy because of its triangular shape and with startlingly good capability. Avro's test pilot, Roly Falk, memorably showed what it could do at the Farnborough Air Show in 1952, handling it like a fighter – not surprising in view of the time and trouble that went into designing it. Finally there was the Victor, in some respects advanced, but lacking the Vulcan's superb manoeuverability.

Like all good things, the posting had to be waited for: a discipline visited so severely on the officer who was the first choice for the job that, after two years in a hanging-about capacity, he finally passed his fly-by date and gave it up. I was the replacement for the famous, heavily decorated and universally popular Ivor Broom, a staff member at Manby who had done much to help me on the course. Amongst his qualities was not drinking. I and others could only marvel at the fortitude he had displayed during years of enduring mess balls and dinners without the analgesia of booze. That virtue was not shared by a fellow student who sat next to me during a dinner marking the end of the course. The main speaker was the loquacious new commandant, Air Commodore Gus Walker. My friend had drunk much too much and had become noisy. To save him from last-minute Nemesis I said to a waiter standing behind us, 'Please bring the wing commander some coffee.'

'Yes, please do,' shouted my intended beneficiary, 'and while you're at it, bring some toast and marmalade.' Gus shut up within seconds.

My wait, much shorter than Ivor's, was a treat in itself. I was to be the wing commander in charge of flying at RAF Waddington, another permanent station and one of the major airfields designated as 'Master Diversion' (MDA), successor to the special relief airfields open during the war to cater for fuel shortages, bad weather or base obstructed by crashes. The job also gave me charge of two resident Canberra bomber squadrons, Nos 37 and 38. With them I was able to get plenty of flying in an aircraft I loved. I did many practice bombing runs, not all that different from those in my wartime tours, dropping small practice bombs on ranges near our Saltfleetby cottage.

Also at Waddington was the Vulcan conversion unit, where crews for the first squadron, numbered 617 after that of the famous Dambusters, were already being trained. The chief instructor was a highly decorated bomber ace, Wing Commander Frank Dodd, an excellent pilot and instructor with gentility of manner that overlaid steely determination. The two of us made a good team under Group Captain Spencer Ring. Above him was the by now Air Vice-Marshal Gus Walker, newly appointed, as Air Officer Commanding 1 Group. The two bomber groups at the time, the numbers kept in being because of their historic importance, were No. 1, known by its arrogant members in a football metaphor as First Division North, and No. 3, known disparagingly as Third Division South. I had come across Walker not only as a long-winded after dinner speaker but also as a noser-around, as opposed to a taker of general interest in the college activities, given to describing mundane things as 'fascinatingly interesting'. As a base commander in Bomber Command during World War Two he had lost his right arm in an attempt to rescue the crew of an aircraft loaded with bombs that had crashed. Critics commented that, had he left the rescue to the trained fire fighters and armourers, he would not have been hurt. Having been a top-class rugger player, he became a referee of the same calibre, and despite his disability he flew with remarkable adaptive skill.

My first direct encounter with him at Waddington was on a night when I was trying to help the confused American pilot of an incoming transatlantic aircraft in bad weather, as part of my job of caring for users of the MDA. Having been told of the possible emergency by his group operations room, Walker turned up in the

Waddington control tower. I, having done my best to reassure the pilot, had positioned him for a radar-guided approach and landing with our very skilled controller, Squadron Leader Peter Jermyn. Walker asked a string of interfering questions. Interrupting his initial instructions to the pilot, Peter, to his great credit, loudly exclaimed: 'I must have utter hush.' He got it; and all was well. For me there was a lot more of Walker to come.

Soon came one of the wider aspects of the general duties (GD) that officers of the flying branch were required to perform. Spencer Ring asked me to take charge of the impending visit to Waddington by the Duchess of Kent. I wrote an elaborate operation and went over the plans with the main participants. The apical item was to be luncheon (lunch not being an elegant enough term) in the officers' mess. It must, we decided, be rehearsed the day before, in its entirety except for the booze. The menu was smoked trout, rack of lamb and, as the awful faux-dainty RAF VIP catering system had it, *'Delice des Dames'* – the last being brought to refreshing reality by Peter Jermyn, the irrepressible, as 'ice cream with bits of Ovaltine in it'. Nothing, however, could deflate the 'Moka' with which we finished (I wondered if it was really Nescafé). And nothing could detract from Jerome Kern, Irving Berlin and Robert Farnon, all featured in the tasteful 'Selections of Music' rendered by the strings of the RAF Central Band.

What could have been a contretemps was down to the extroverted Sir Harry Broadhurst, Commander-in-Chief of Bomber Command, who had joined the company of dancers of attendance. Knowing better than the airman whose job it was, he ushered the royal aircraft to a point between the hangars from which it would be almost inextricable, saving the royal party a yard or two of walking but not my nails from several nanometres of biting. We pulled it clear with a tractor. All else went well. I was smothered with thanks. And the officers' mess, like all those that hosted female royals, got a refurbished ladies' lavatory.

I spent the weekends at the house we had been given at Finningley, the station, permanent yet again, where my squadron, numbered after the famous and long-established First World War unit 101, was to form. The airfield had just been refurbished and there was rubble and rubbish everywhere. As Gregor and I bicycled across it towards the adjoining village, he fell, revealing as I picked him up a huge cut in his thigh from a bit of airfield lighting broken glass. I waved down a van in the middle distance, which came to the rescue and took us to the sick bay. As the doctor sewed it up, it proved to be no more than a flesh wound but there was a lot of blood. I fainted, waking to the doctor's stentorian cry to the orderly to, 'Do something about the wing commander.' Rachel, of course, was present as the twentieth stitch went in. Her maternal, 'What do you say?' got a moving filial, 'Thank you' from Gregor.

The house was a pre-war married quarter for a senior officer. Fortunately, we had a batman to help with the huge task of keeping it in order. We were also blessed with a good school in Doncaster for Gregor. For David, now ensconced at Ardingly, I was able to keep up the three-weekly parental visits in an Anson borrowed from Waddington, flying to the MDA at Thorney Island and going by train to the school's nearest town, Haywards Heath.

In July I left my job to become Frank Dodd's student on the Vulcan, using my last few Canberra trips to try out the new, semi-automated radar descent instrument landing scheme (ILS), precursor to hands-off versions that later came into general use. With Frank's help I found the Vulcan amenable and a joy to fly. The brilliant control system, so sensitive that it had to be fitted with artificial 'feel', made pilots forget its enormous size and although far more complicated technically than any aircraft I had come across before, simple once one got the hang. In unbounded exhilaration, I could hardly believe my luck. Never mind the career, I thought, just let me get on with the job.

My inheritance was no mean one. The first role of 101 Squadron was night bombing in the FE2B, a canvas-and-string stalwart of the First World War, under the command of the sonorously named Major the Honourable Twistelton-Wykeham-Fiennes. Thereafter mothballed, 101 re-formed at the famous Norfolk base, Bircham Newton, in 1928. It was equipped first with Sidestrand and later

Overstrand aircraft, still partly canvas and with wires instead of string. The Sidestrand sported a scarf ring, a horizontal circular mount for swivelling the Vickers gas-operated machine gun by hand. The Overstrand had the first Boulton Paul power-operated turret, later armed with four Browning machine guns to become a standard fitment. Named after Norfolk villages, the aircraft survive in silver modelled form amongst the squadron's treasures.

Re-equipped with Blenheim light bombers, 101 took part in the notoriously dangerous daylight raids envisaged as feasible by the pre-war air staff but soon abandoned because of crushing losses. Converting to Wellingtons, the squadron was part of the 1,000 bomber force scraped together for raids on Berlin and Essen, more for the sake of British civilian morale than for damaging those cities. Re-equipped again with Lancasters, 101 paved the way for the air-borne landings in Normandy by flattening houses obstructing one of the dropping zones on which, among thousands of others, I later dropped.

After a spell in the job of electronic jamming of German anti-aircraft radar, the squadron resumed daylight bombing. With the Luftwaffe on its last legs, the opposition was inconsiderable. When, after the armistice, Bomber Command joined the transport force to drop food to the Dutch and bring home prisoners of war, the squadron took part. Following a six-year stint with Lincoln bombers, 101 became a jet bomber unit, using their Canberras in the catastrophic Suez campaign in 1956 and later against communist terrorists in Malaya.

Now came the Vulcan. The prospects could not have been more exciting, but the foreground was dismal. We chafed at the slow emergence of the new aircraft from the Avro airfield at Woodford, near their main Chadderton factory. The ground crews were still learning how to maintain the few we had and the serviceability was terrible. The elaborate facilities needed for a V Force station were far from complete except for the new 3,000 yard runway flat to within a few inches and the object of visits by admiring engineers. We managed, somehow, to start on long navigation exercises and practice bombing runs over special radar measurement sites capable of very precise assessment of our accuracy. There were frequent practices of action in the event of war consisting of hurried dispersals to designated airfields scattered over the UK. More demandingly we practised emergency take-offs from Finningley in response to a hypothetical crisis so sudden that dispersal would have been impossible. That usually meant leaping from bed, struggling into flying kit, jumping into the waiting cars and thence into the cockpit, starting all four engines at once and rocketing off the runway: all forming so compressed a sequence as to make it seem like a single movement. The scrambles, comparable to those of Battle of Britain pilots, were exhilarating. We became so proficient that on one occasion I was still strapping in as we passed through 30,000 feet on the way to our 50,000 feet operating height. There was a real sense of dedication as we refined the procedures, encouraged by the build-up, at last, to our complement of eight aircraft. It showed in the practice bombing results and the keenness with which we embarked on the rigorous Bomber Command categorization scheme, a ladder with 'Combat' at the bottom, ascending by way of 'Select' to the rarefied 'Select Star'.

Finningley soon acquired as station commander Group Captain Douglas Haig, another Battle of Britain veteran. He knew little of the bomber business but was very supportive. His right-hand man was the chief administrator, James 'Mouse' Grant. I had as one flight commander Squadron Leader Norman Wilkins, highly unusual in that he was a navigator whom I had selected in preference to a pilot because, though overanxious to please, he was keen and competent.

The other flight was run by Johnnie Walker, free of his name's boozy implication. An RAF rugger team player from New Zealand, he too was keen and competent. In my crew was the radar navigator and bomb-releaser Vic Rollason, assiduous at the hours of target study that accurate results demanded; and as conventional navigator, Bob Harbour, like my former navigator, Sergeant Bolton, a town planner with meticulous skill. I used a variety of second pilots chosen from the other captains and, having qualified as a Vulcan instrument rating examiner, used the tests for ordinary supervisory flying. My charges soon learnt that taxiing the aircraft without allowing the wheels at the centre to move was a category-busting offence, along with leaving the massive cockpit windscreen wipers on when it wasn't raining.

I had doubts about inviting non-Vulcan pilots as guest second pilot because of a major accident that caused a total loss before the aircraft entered squadron service. Squadron Leader 'Podge' Howard, very experienced in multifarious types, was landing at Heathrow. He had as second pilot Air Marshal Sir Harry Broadhurst. The final stages of his approach went wrong and on Sir Harry's order they used their ejection seats and escaped. The two navigators were left behind and killed: their only means of escape was by ordinary parachute through the door hatch and the aircraft was too close to the ground for that. The inquiry found that Podge had acted correctly. I made an exception of Duggie Haig, who, very keen to take part, soon picked up enough to make a useful second pilot.

We improved in fits and starts. Just as we reckoned ourselves to be a going concern, six inches of snow covered the airfield. We were supposed to be an all-weather force and I decided to try out the small wheels of the Vulcan undercarriage, so far as I knew for the first time, on a snowy runway at night. When my flight plan reached the Group operations room, Wing Commander Paddy Finch, an air staff officer and friend, ordered me not to take off because of the snow. When he admitted that Gus Walker had not been consulted and that he had made the decision, I sniffily reminded him that as squadron commander the decision was mine and I was ignoring his order. Off we went. After a few acutely anxious seconds and some whooshing, the Vulcan, accelerating comparatively slowly, took to the air with its usual grace. Towards the end of a five-hour flight the control centre told me that, as forecast, the whole of the UK was blanketed in low cloud. He offered me as diversion airfields Lossiemouth, still a naval station alongside the Moray Firth, which is often blessed with an anomaly of good weather, or the US Libyan base at Wheelus, near Tripoli. I chose Lossiemouth. While we were on the descent from 50,000 feet even Morayshire closed in, reaching a state in which, by the book, we could not land. As Wheelus was now out of range, our situation looked a little bleak. Beginning my ground-controlled approach, I realized that the naval controller was highly skilled and that he and I had the same sort of compatibility as I had enjoyed with another controller, George Harding, at Nutts Corner.

The approach, with all due immodesty, was flawless, also doing him great credit because he was accustomed to small Buccaneer aircraft. In thick snow, just as his talk-down was ending with a satisfying sequence of 'steady ... steady', he suddenly said, 'You're 25 feet high [above the glide path].'

I felt obliged to ask, 'Which bit of the aircraft are you aiming at? The Vulcan's 26 feet tall.'

Before he could answer we landed routinely. The captain station commander, who had got out of bed to be present at what could have been a major accident, enjoyed the joke and complimented us both. I heard no more of my contretemps with Paddy.

I felt sad and a little guilty a few days later about a serious Vulcan accident because it might have been a consequence of my own adventure. My erstwhile Vulcan instructor Frank Dodd, landing at Waddington on a snowy runway, swerved into a bank of piled-up snow close to the tarmac edge. The damage was serious but nobody was hurt. Like my glider mishap at White Waltham, his error was long remembered:

You shouldn't have put the Vulcan in the bank, Frank.

It would have been uncharacteristic of Frank to have tried a 'me too'. Perhaps he simply wanted to confirm my result.

As Christmas 1957 approached I anticipated a practice alert during the holiday, so that group headquarters could satisfy themselves that our state of readiness remained unaffected. Before lunch on Christmas Eve, when the non-emergency part of the station had closed, I found Duggie Haig and Mouse Grant in the officers' mess bar, both drinking. That made me the only sober senior GD (flying branch) officer available to take charge of an alert for a take-off, which I would myself lead. Fortunately, nothing happened. Neither

101

of the revellers reacted to my decision, more from funk than compassion, not to shop them, as I should have done.

Before we had finished welding ourselves together as a unit we had to divert effort to the displays for which our beautiful white giants were ideal and much in demand. (They were white because that was the best colour to reflect the heat and radioactivity that would ensue after the release of a nuclear weapon.) One daunting job, to which all hands had to turn until better means came along, was to use rags and polish to keep them gleaming. Another was the mostly unproductive flying involved. We took part in many Battle of Britain commemoration days at bases scattered across the UK, covering half a dozen in an afternoon, with fly-pasts at low level and soaraways into the blue or grey, as the case might be. The four Bristol Olympus 6 engines – prototypes, incidentally, for those of Concord – were quiet enough in the cockpit, but when they gave their all, the noise outside was not so much loud as seemingly flattening of everything around.

Overseas commitments gobbled up resources but were great fun. They also oiled the diplomatic wheels of giving away a bit of the Empire, a process in spate at the time. To celebrate the freedom of Nigeria, I flew a Vulcan overnight to Kano, landing early enough to minimize the local hazard of bird strike from vultures. That, plus the local solution of piles of carrion for the birds' edification, kept them away from the approach, did the trick. The snag was the presence of Gus Walker. His presence seemed connected with the dancing of attendance on the Duke of Gloucester at Kaduna to represent the queen as the Union flag was lowered and the gaudy Nigerian flag was raised. Gus's endless questions and needless warnings were tiresome but didn't spoil the fly-over of the main Nigerian towns. One was Sokoto, where we landed at the request of the local ruler, the Sirdana – comparable with the Fakir of Ipi of staff college days, but friendly. Using his Oxford-educated son as interpreter, he asked how much a Vulcan would cost. On being told £3.25 million plus £600,000 for the radar, he commented that buying one would add a quarter to his people's income tax. No sale.

The squadron attended, as a three-aircraft detachment, a similar ceremony at another former outpost – Kenya, where the opening of the new airport at Embakasi was to be part of the fun. I landed there first. In view of the apparent immensity of the new runway I decided not to bother with streaming the tail parachute normally used to help to bring the Vulcan to a halt; thereby saving us from having to complete a chore done at base by the ground crew and not within local competence. What I failed to reckon with was the height of Embakasi above sea level – 6,000 feet, thus the highest in Africa and most of the world. That meant that our true landing speed would be some 20 knots higher than normal. I touched down accurately at the threshold, but we ran the whole enormous length, finishing with smoke from the brakes, of which I was asking too much. As we taxied majestically to the stopping point where the dignitaries were arrayed, a stroppy controller told me that we had in tow the cables of the lighting system stretching for hundreds of yards behind us. Our arrival thus got something short of a standing ovation. To be fair, the cables should have been buried, but that, I felt, would not be an ice-cutting excuse. Fortunately, we were scheduled to leave almost at once. That we did, leaving the air attaché to do the explaining.

Another air attaché had some explaining to do for himself at a later port of call – Saigon – where we were celebrating the freedom of South Vietnam, brief though it proved to be, between French colonial rule and American occupation. When we arrived we were terribly surprised to find that, while the runways were strong enough to bear the weight of Vulcans, the taxiways were not. At terrible inconvenience to our hosts, who were nonetheless polite and welcoming, we parked, refuelled and did our servicing on a runway. There was general delight with our displays except for the USAF contingent, whose C124 and C130 transports lumbering across the sky we eclipsed. They, like us, had an eye on the market potential of the dignitaries from China, the Philippines, Japan, Korea, Malaysia and others invited to the do.

The best of these jaunts was a transatlantic one done in partnership with a Victor squadron commander mellifluously named Ulick

Burberry. We gave joint displays, starting at the annual (later biennial) air show at Farnborough organized by the Society of British Aircraft Constructors (later British Aerospace Contractors). I had long been used to bringing Anson-loads of Cranwell and CFS friends to the show, landing at nearby Blackbushe, later famous as Greenham Common. But the fact that I was taking part in the display myself was new and exciting. I did two fast runs a few feet above the runway with a tightly banked circuit between. On each run the Vulcan was garlanded with little clouds of water vapour on the upper wing, caused by cooling in the low-pressure areas on which lift depended, as Dr Kermode had taught me long ago. We clambered away, hampered by the fuel load needed to reach Toronto, site of the next display. The announcer told the crowd that the time change would enable us to get there before we had left Farnborough. Ulick and his Victor, with much shorter range, had to drop in at Goose Bay, for many years a refuelling stop for aircraft en route from Britain.

We too had fuel problems. Toronto control had not been told of my trip and the controller ordered me to conform to the ordinary approach procedure and wait in the holding pattern. After a minor wrangle he got the message and ushered me straight to the waterfront for a fly-past and landing, gasping for fuel, at the nearby RCAF base at Trenton. I doubted whether there would be enough to taxi in, but we made it.

The fault for what could have been a sticky end was that of the officer supposed to be in charge of the joint venture, Group Captain 'Johnnie' Johnson. He was the greatest of all the Battle of Britain aces, draped in DSOs, DFCs and bars. He greeted us somewhat over-effusively; nervous because he knew nothing about V Force aircraft and, as was clear from the absence of preparation, our arrival for the job in hand. Having got himself the job simply as a jolly, he made no useful contribution – a pity, because I could have done with some help with the Trenton locals. They, understandably, were pre-occupied with their own display team, the superb Golden Hawks, comparable to the RAF Red Arrows. Ulick and I had the task, on each of the three display days, of doing two sea-level high-speed runs in opposite directions along the waterfront, interspersed by steep pull-ups to 5,000 feet and sharp wing-overs and diving turns to point us at each other again. We passed as close to each other as we dared: having discovered that 'Toronto' is native for 'meeting', I was perhaps more than usually concerned to avoid one with Ulick's Victor. The displays were not entirely suited to taking in the view en route but I enjoyed, at the top of the southerly turns, glimpses of the Niagara Falls in the far distance. We were too busy at Trenton to see round Toronto, but we were invited to an elaborate dinner, curiously named 'complimentary' by Toronto's city fathers (and mothers) and attended by the mayor and eighteen aldermen and women.

The menu varied from the norm with leather beef instead of rubber chicken. The head of the Canadian National Industrial Exhibition, sponsors of the whole affair, was lyrical in his speech about us as stealers of the show from the US and Russian participants and even the Golden Hawks. Less delighted was another speaker, General Curtis LeMay, former head of USAF Strategic Air Command (SAC), our competitors for prestige.

As a small and relaxing overseas perk we were allowed a continuation of a long-standing Bomber Command custom known as Lone Ranger. Having hogged several of the glamorous duty destinations I chose a humble trip to El Adem, one of the Western Desert airfields that I had known so well in the 1940s, near the Mediterranean coast and beautiful in its own way. It was now a well-developed staging post for short-range aircraft on delivery to Middle East customers. My recollection of the hospitality and the self-maintenance that was part of the exercise was clouded by copious quantities of Orangeboom, a deceptively powerful Dutch beer. But I'm sure I had a good time.

All these diversions did not prevent a steady improvement in serviceability as we learnt the Vulcan's snags and foibles and in bombing accuracy and the speed with which we completed practice take-offs. Vic Rollason's devoted target study, and doubtless a bit of luck, led on a memorable night in January 1959 to an almost unheard-of achievement on a radar target – a direct hit. More typically, our errors were in the low hundreds of yards. All the striving for accuracy was partly a leftover from the age of conventional bombing, and partly to allow for the possibility, remote as we thought, but later to materialize during the Falklands War, of a reversion to the conventional role when a Vulcan damaged the airfield with the only bomb ever released from a Vulcan in war. The technique, moreover, was used for the annual Bomber Command bombing competition. There, like elephants dropping rabbit currants, we showered the ranges near Saltfleetby with 11lb practice bombs.

Chapter 16

Strengthening the Deterrent

In parallel, we worked away at our proper job. There emerged, like Whittle's jet at Cranwell, the object of our main efforts – the Hydrogen bomb, housed in new buildings remote from most others on the airfield. It was like a huge green dustbin, filling our capacious bomb bays. Some of the details are still classified and the Official Secrets Act may thus apply. It is safe to reveal, however, that it was handled not by RAF armourers, but by white-coated boffins from the Atomic Weapons Research Establishment, later to become infamous as Aldermaston. Much time having passed, it is also safe to disclose the weapon's code name, which was 'Yellow Sun', one of many assigned to miscellaneous weaponry. A classic was 'Red Dean', doubly appropriate because Hewlett Johnson, a notorious cleric with communist leanings, was neatly matched with the rocket he doubtless received from on high. Others were the 'Fat Boy' and 'Tall Boy' labels used for the original atom bombs.

The boffins duly hauled the dustbin into position, fiddling with thickets of cable and gizmoid linkages. They then left us to practise the arming and release procedures in the air; dauntingly complex but, we were assured, to be made much simpler in the production models. A main prototype safety device, allegorical, as I thought, was a huge quantity of stainless steel balls, protecting the core mechanism from damage or premature release. Their use chimed with the RAF testicular slang for a technical cock-up: a 'Hoffmans', after the famous firm that made ball bearings for a variety of aircraft.

We continued to strive assiduously for accuracy in our radar-assisted bombing runs. I had, however, come across an estimate in Singapore of the probable area of destruction of a Soviet weapon of the same order of magnitude as our own. A hit on London, it indicated, would devastate a circular area with a radius extending to Preston (North End, I surmised, in a marginal note meant to leaven the awesome solemnity of the study; Preston North End is, of course, a well-known football club). The estimate seemed to make errors of the sort we were used to inconsequential and our efforts to minimize them nugatory. We accepted that lobbing weapons of mass destruction any old where was not good enough, but there was no need for the accuracy that was our goal. Trying to achieve it became a chore.

Not so another form of practice. Fighter affiliation required protracted flying, straight and level, at heights that suited the fighters using the time-hallowed technique of quarter attacks, curving inwards from the flanks until they were directly astern and affording them as long a period as possible for aiming and releasing their missiles. Such were the Vulcan's performance and manoeuverability, however, that we were relieved from boredom by a reversal of roles. The fighters did the straight and level, and we did the attacking. This game, much enjoyed by all, ended when one of the Javelin fighter station commanders felt it demeaning and bad for pilot morale for a huge aircraft to simulate their role and occasionally out-perform them.

Immune from such challenges were practice emergencies in co-operation with the Master Diversion Airfields, of which my former perch at Waddington was one. An incident that happened in reality from time to time, particularly in Meteors and Canberras, was the simulated engine failure known as the flame-out. The MDA's technique for getting single and double flame-out victims was well rehearsed. Thinking that my friends there might like a change, I electrified Waddington control one night by asking, probably for the first time, for assistance with a practice quadruple flame-out. I could picture what was happening in the control tower during the brief silence, after which the situation received the calm and efficient treatment I had hoped for as we drifted downwards with four engines throttled back. Though remote, the possibility was not entirely credible. And trying it out in the flight simulator had shown that if the Vulcan ditched, its performance would be satisfactory.

What, tragically, was beyond redemption was the gross electrical failure that caused a freezing of the controls and a fatal dive by an aircraft from 617 Squadron on a liaison visit to the US. The accident led to extensive modification of the Vulcan electrical system, said to have been powerful enough to light a small town. Mechanical failure, however, was an even rarer cause of accidents in the Vulcan than it was in other aircraft. The common bugbear of pilot error prevailed, as in the sad instance of Squadron Leader Tony Smailes, a friend and RAF rugger player from 617 Squadron, whose Vulcan clipped a small obstruction short of a runway in New Zealand. The aircraft was a complete wreck. He was so upset that he left the RAF. I thought of the naval tale of the captain of a destroyer escort of an aircraft carrier who crashed his ship, at night in mid-Atlantic, into the carrier's side and sheered away. The infuriated carrier captain signalled: 'What are your intentions?' receiving the reply, 'I'm going to buy a farm.'

Tony and the captain had a predecessor. A courtier, bowing low before Queen Elizabeth I, broke wind. Such was his shame and remorse that he retired to his country seat and felt unable to return to court for many years. Plucking up courage at last, he returned and made obeisance. 'Welcome back,' said Her Majesty, 'I did forget the fart.'

Frank Dodd, to return to the subject in hand, had obliged by renewing my Instrument Rating Examiner qualification on the Vulcan. The tests I was thereby qualified to conduct were a good way of keeping up standards without prolonged sittings in the second pilot's seat with a virtual clipboard. Each test had to include 'recovery from unusual positions,' which required the examiner to throw the aircraft about, finishing in some awkward posture. The candidate, whom one hoped would have been disoriented as he would have been in a real upset, had then to restore the aircraft to an even keel solely by the use of instruments, plus such seat-of-the-pants ability as he might possess. Trying to do that, one second pilot made what the trade calls opposite corrections, thereby making matters worse. Having come to the rescue too late, I could not prevent our speed in a dive from exceeding Mach 0.87 (M1.0 being, of course, the speed of sound or sound barrier, the former being the Vulcan's limit. Fearful that I had made the aircraft unfit for use by overstressing it, I used the old boy system – for once, as I thought justified. I rang up Mike Harrison, an old friend from Charterhouse and assistant chief pilot at A.V. Roe (Avro), makers of the Vulcan. He reassured me with the news that 0.87 was a limit imposed by the RAF. Avro were confident that their aircraft could withstand a much higher figure. My bacon, not to mention my job, was safe. *Floreat aeternum Carthusiana Domus* (what is not prudence is danger).

One of my later instrument rating candidates was Gus Walker himself. His one-armed instrument flying in the Vulcan was as good as it was in the Canberra, the other aircraft in his Group. I was relieved to be able to give him, in good conscience, a rating that he used, no doubt, for the self-promotion at which he was so adept. I also made myself useful keeping pilots with single-engined experience in practice in the runabout Chipmunk trainer, in which I also did part of the job of giving the local air cadet members air experience. Waddington continued to favour me with the loan of their Anson for more weekend visits to Thorney Island for take-outs from Ardingly. I was always grateful to the wing commander in charge of flying there for never asking why an experienced Vulcan pilot was as much in need as I seemed to be of weekend Anson navigation and sometimes GCA practice at his airfield.

The arrival at Finningley of a second squadron made life more interesting. It was the old-established No. 83, equipped with Valiant four-jet bombers, the first and least satisfactory component of the V Force. But a Valiant had the distinction of having dropped the prototype British nuclear bomb at Christmas Island in the Pacific; a doubtful achievement perhaps, because the radioactive fallout did terrible harm to the people on the ground, some in trouble for years afterwards. The dropper, incidentally, was Squadron Leader Arthur Steele, a former associate examiner at CFS. The risk at Finningley was a jealously based disharmony between the two squadrons. I was lucky to start a good relationship when, returning from an air test, I came across a stray Valiant, short of fuel and too low to use its many location devices to find the airfield. I earned useful points for shepherding it home.

Chapter 17

Through Adversity

As my tour neared its end, two events interacted to fuel my doubts. First came an official visit from a junior minister, from what was still the Air Ministry, called Orr-Ewing, later the Lord of that ilk. After seeing round the elaborate Operations Room and supervising Finningley's part of a nuclear strike, the spacious new crew's dressing rooms and showers, he addressed all of the air crews in the briefing hall. He praised the labours that had made us operational. He exulted in the prestige that came from Britain having a nuclear strike force of her own, and thanked us for our part in creating it. He stressed that we were just in time, leaving us in no doubt that, at the drop of a hat, we could be on our way to deal with the looming Soviet threat to our country. Such was his gung-ho nationalism that he seemed blind to the realities of what the consequences of a nuclear strike and retaliation could be. He seemed in denial of the nuclear pawn in the deterrent game that Britain was. Uncurling my toes, I helped to usher him back to political cloud cuckoo land.

Following that occasion came a revelation from Paddy Finch, our row about the snowy runway long forgotten. The Orr-Ewing visits to us and the other V Force stations had to do with a forthcoming statement to the House of Commons. The terrible delays in bringing the V Force into being had generated political pressure for a ministerial assurance that the British Nuclear Deterrent was ready for action. Domestic politics, not the Soviet Union, had created the urgency. We were the victim of a fraud. Silly me, I thought, for thinking we were serving the country. And if there was no urgency for the 'deterrent', did we really need it at all?

Coincident with that denouement was a period deficient of enough to occupy my bookish mind. I needed something to bite on: perhaps a qualification that would serve me well if I stayed in the RAF or come in handy if I left. I remembered that the only residual benefit of my father having made me take the Edinburgh First MB was the matriculation to London University that came with it. I asked the registrar whether I could change from medicine (long abandoned) to law. The answer was yes. With the support of the admirable RAF Education Service and the Metropolitan College of Law, I embarked on a correspondence course for the external degree of Bachelor of Law. It was slow, absorbing, intellectual pabulum that kept me going for years, not least on long Vulcan trips when I used case reports written on cards to prepare for the practice exams, which I took periodically, for the Metropolitan College to correct.

There were other sources of delight, one of which was a seductive affair with the Victor – another V bomber like the Vulcan. A joint project with another squadron commander, Wing Commander Mike Beetham (subsequently to rise to the rank of Marshal of the RAF – now rarefied because the rank has been abolished) chimed neatly with a game played in the officers' mess after dinner by opposing teams on the mess carpet. The protagonist, lying blindfold and armed with a rolled-up newspaper, would try to locate and swipe the antagonist, relying solely on the answer 'Yes' to the question: 'Are you there Moriarty?' A successful hit-scoring point led to reversal of roles. For Mike and me the carpet was an area of the Atlantic Ocean and the newspaper a V bomber; his a Victor and mine a Vulcan.

In what were very early trials of how to effect long-range inter-ceptions for flight refuelling, we established that getting close enough to put short-range location equipment to use was not unduly difficult: our repetitions of the question being, as we hoped, a source of mystification to transatlantic air traffic controllers unfamiliar with RAF quirks. Flight refuelling, incidentally, had a long history, which began in 1929 with Douglas C1 biplane tankers and Fokker recipients. No doubt the same ribald comparisons with sexual encounters were being made. Early pioneers included Sir Alan Cobham, he of the air display circus that was the genesis of my interest in aviation. The same job was done by 101 Squadron (at one time commanded by me) equipped with VC10s converted from passenger to fuel carrying.

Our final burst of activity as a crew was to get as much practice as possible for the forthcoming Bomber Command bombing competition. The year before, we had come nowhere, not because of any shortcomings, but rather from my own enforced neglect. Worse still, we had not been selected to compete in the Bomber Command contest with Strategic Air Command at Orlando, Florida. Determined to do better this time I somehow fitted in a lot of practice. In the competition we came, to our delight, eighth out of the 200-plus competing crews. Our errors were 310, 50 and 210 yards for the first three 'bombs'; but the fourth was 7 miles off because of a technical fault. But for that we might well have won. This was a source of great satisfaction, tinged with a renewal of my nagging doubt about the point of striving for accuracy in delivering bombs of nuclear destructive power, but in no way did it detract from the kudos of the award to our crew of the coveted 'Select Star' category. I handed over command of the squadron, elated by the superb flying experience of the previous two years, but cast down by the dishonesty of the politicians, amounting, as I saw it, of falsification to the point of forgery.

My next appointment was to the Directing Staff (DS) of the Joint Services Staff College (JSSC). This middle-ranking establishment, a stepping stone for some to the Imperial Defence College for the very senior, was sited at a grand rather than stately country house in the hamlet of Latimer, near Chesham. Its object was to familiarize students with the other services, the higher direction of defence and Britain's strategic place in the world, thereby fitting them for joint staff posts. The clientele included Commonwealth and American officers.

One of the former whom I welcomed particularly was a Canadian wing commander, Al Mackie, having as another similarity to me a transport background in the RCAF. We both contemplated with amused anticipation the oddities and confusions that might follow.

I had joined the DS without having had to do the course, which was not unique in College history but highly unusual. My worry about not being up to my job soon faded. I found no difficulty in getting on or keeping up with the rest of the faculty and with the students, some brighter than their mentors. The visiting lecturers were much better than they had been at Bracknell, as were most of the exercises. Paradoxically, the worst constraint was the grating and inhibiting inter-service pseudo-bonhomie. So anxious were we all to appear 'joint', that such challenging of one service by another as there was seemed half-hearted. To this collective anxiety was the added pressure to toe the party line. At plenary sessions I found the same easily perceived orthodoxy for the sake of subliminal self-promotion that had been obtained, much more justifiably, at the RAF Selection Board and the single-service Staff College.

One remarkable figure at the JSSC was the Commandant, Air Vice-Marshal Sir Laurence Sinclair: gifted, percipient and almost a professional commandant because of the number of other establishments over which he had presided. His wisdom in defence affairs was lost when he retired to run the United Kingdom Air Traffic Control Service.

The services took it in turns to provide commandants, and his successor was Vice Admiral Jack Scatchard, known inappropriately as Jolly Jack, whose reign was placid. Dutifully he asked the staff and their wives to dinner, ending the dinner with parlour games. One cold evening Rachel and I, with the other guests, braced ourselves for the post-prandial ordeal of three-dimensional noughts and crosses played on a plastic gizmo. As we were about to start, the large and ancient Scatchard dog came to the rescue with a fart so suffocatingly malodorous that there was nothing for it but to abandon ship. Seldom can an apology have been accepted with such alacrity as Jack's. The dog should have had a rosette: appropriately positioned, of course.

We were glad to get home early to the small house in the walled garden that we had accepted in preference to the standard married quarters because the rent was less. It suited us admirably, as did Latimer's location, not unduly far from Ardingly and Rachel's beloved West Country.

Scatchard's deputy, appointed on a Buggins' turn basis from the longest serving four-stripe senior DS member, was Group Captain Nick Carter, formerly Air Attaché to the Lebanon and said to have answered their request for a classical motto for the Lebanese Air Force crest with the *nil illegitimi carborundum* that I had used so successfully as a staff college student. He was engaging, studious, funny and a member of the very select circle of writers on military affairs; ideally suited for the job. He was soon promoted and left, to be replaced by the agreeable Hugh Disney. The other bright star was Rex Whitworth, an outstanding intellectual Guard's officer. As we departed for one of our three-day weekends he, fond of awful jokes, was heard to quote from a hymn (Ancient & Modern 545):

Fading is the world's best pleasure.

The senior sailor, Captain Bailey, was on the point of retiring – or, as he put it, choking with emotion when the day came, 'striking my pennant.' During what I thought were the really important tutorial discussions, on nuclear warfare and the so-called British Independent Deterrent then due to be transferred from the V Force to Trident submarines, he came out against it. His reasoning was pragmatic: he and other submariners, he thought, would not fancy being hove-to off the North Cape for months at a time. That, for him, was clinching and conclusive. It seemed to me quaint and worrying that he, supposedly well acquainted with strategic issues, should have regarded so shallow an argument as resolving so profound an issue. His successor was Captain Bromley Martin, a little more intelligent but the butt of the lower orders' habit of nicknaming: the 'Bromley', in his case, giving place to 'Remy'.

Some of the rest of us were less well 'identified', as I had known it at the RAF Selection Board, with our respective services. A soldier, the delightful Lieutenant Colonel The Lord ('Reggie') Lydford, thought of little other than getting back to his West Country farm. An airman colleague, impatient with his job, looked forward to running the family-owned laundry in Norfolk. Having been deceived in my Vulcan days, I was wary of accepting the givens dinned into the staff and students alike. I could but be suspicious of the JSSC and all its works.

That attitude I overdid, losing me points and making it hard to get what I said taken seriously. I railed particularly against the use of DS time to micro-plan an exercise involving an airborne and air-transported assault on part of the Arabian Peninsula, aptly named Hotpoint by Rex Whitworth. Another RAF DS member with whom I had served before ran true to form, cooing his brown-nosed approval of what his seniors said and doing the fiddly, time-wasting jobs correctly. I, disapproving and surly, did mine carelessly and wrongly. I thought of A.A. Milne's two bears. Good Bear, blast him, was immaculate and well behaved. But 'Bad Bear's knicker ties were terribly tore.'

Good Bear decorated his married quarter with squadron shields, bought mugs, ties and RAF paraphernalia, and agreed throughout his career with all the right people. He rose to Air Chief Marshal rank and did a prominent RAF-linked civilian job before the cancer that killed his wife did for him as well.

Bad Bear used the excellent college library to delve more deeply into the strategy underpinning the alleged case for a British nuclear deterrent. Most of the maps used to put that case, I saw, were Mercator projection depictions of the world laid flat, distorting the northern and southern extremities by enlargement. The result was a Britain literally writ large; about the same size as India, for instance, instead of the true size ratio of about 1:6. Another distortion was to depict Britain as poised between the two great land masses of America and Euro-Asia, instead of the small offshore island of Europe that it actually is. The two distortions together fostered the illusion of Britain's greatness and importance; just the vote-getting nostrum that an electorate whose pride had been hurt by the loss of an empire and post-war economic decline would lap up.

Churchill, in his 1946 speech at Fulton Missouri, had coined the phrase 'Cold War'. From this flowed the notion that the Soviet Union was on the march and that their hordes might cross the Channel at any moment (little less grotesque, perhaps, than the ludicrous First World War rumour that Russian troops had been seen in England with snow still on their boots). How better could Britain regain her standing and prestige than by guarding her shores, buttressed by the atomic weapon that we had invented but had had to hand over to America to develop? Perish the thought, the nuclear lore seemed to proclaim, that the Soviet empire felt no less threatened than its American and later NATO opponent. And never let it be disclosed that Britain's bomb, far from being a deterrent, fostered the very threat it was supposed to forefend, to say nothing of its huge cost and consequent ebbing away of funding much needed for her so-called conventional defence forces.

There were no opportunities for discussing such issues. It was accepted as axiomatic that Britain's forces should remain much as they had been in the glory days of the Empire – a sentiment echoing that of the Duke of Cambridge (head of the Army for decades in the nineteenth century) that nothing should change. Symbolically, perhaps, his remains are set in the stone of his statue in Whitehall. Nowadays, the thinking is much the same. The Army, bristling with main battle tanks of questionable use in any foreseeable circumstance, must be ready to fight a major air/land battle in Europe that could never happen again. The Royal Navy, cut to the bone, must use what's left of the fleet in an attempt to do many of the tasks that are unnecessary now that we are no longer a world maritime power. The RAF must be ready to re-fight the Battle of Britain. Above all, Britain must continue the obeisance to the US that began when we depended on American sustenance to survive the Second World War; now, paradoxically, even more vital because, without American maintenance and navigation, our so-called independent nuclear totem could not operate. Instead of considering such issues, contributing to the pro and anti debate, and even adding pabulum to the discussion, we are almost always confined to patsy questions and, as Wordsworth called them, 'old, unhappy, far-off things and battles long ago', such as an extensive analysis, complete with a lecture room-sized relief map of the German invasion of Norway in 1940. I could not help but regard this as being out of date and stuck in a rut.

Strolling home I found myself wondering about the value of this leisurely talking shop, which could, with sufficient rich productive mess of argument, have made a constructive addition to defence thought. Instead, constricted by another form of politics, what it did was not so much a forgery of the Vulcan kind, as a masquerade. In my final summer (not of consent) in the walled garden, a 100-yard parade of glorious multi-coloured dahlias, I felt growing doubt about whether I still wanted to be part of defence at all. For the present, however, I was moving onward and upward. Back in the intelligence community I had so much enjoyed in the Far East, I was to join, as a group captain, the Joint Intelligence Committee Secretariat in London, disillusioned by forgery and tempered in the experiential forge.

Chapter 18

Policy and Peril

'*Experto crede*' (believe one who has had experience in the matter), as the proverb puts it, taught me to be wary of what my new job might involve as I crossed Westminster Bridge on my first morning. As I did so, my bowler hat – de *rigueur* for Whitehall warriors – was blown by a gust of wind into the Thames, evoking a sympathetic, 'Oh, you poor thing', from a passing lady commuter. Reaching the northern bank, I enjoyed the inscription on the Victorian statue of Boadicea:

> *Regions Caesar never knew*
> *Thy posterity shall sway*

... which, of course, it did, and later didn't, leaving us all with the misguided notion of Britain's place in the world and the root cause of many of our troubles.

On the previous day I had run into the unforeseen hurdle of an interview with the Secretary of State for Air, one Julian Amery, in the Ministry of Defence. Ushered into the presence, I got a glare and was then asked an inconsequential question and ushered out. His object must have been to establish that my suit fitted and that I could talk proper. His own drawl was not quite plummy, more like chucking-out time at the Carlton Club. Discourtesy among the high-ups was rare on that gladsome morning, when all I had to do was find the so-called New Government Buildings, a turn-of-the-century office block in Great George Street.

I duly found my office in the Joint Intelligence Committee Secretariat, which, as Deputy Secretary, I shared with three assistants. One was a seconded member of the Joint Intelligence Bureau, which existed to collect and collate facts and had offices in London and Melbourne. Another was a young member of MI5, the security service dealing with domestic matters. The third, a lieutenant colonel in the Army Intelligence Corps, was the only other serving officer in the Cabinet Office. All three were highly competent and a delight to work with, each in charge of secretarial service for a segment of the Committee's work.

My senior was the secretary of the JIC itself, confusingly ranked as an assistant secretary and thus equitable with a naval commodore, an army brigadier and an air commodore. He was John Hunt, an archetypal chilly civil servant. He was, nevertheless, welcoming, and soon helped me into harness. I was the only four-striper (colonel, captain RN or group captain) seconded member; and, in common with everybody else, free from any of the political pressures that later plagued the JIC and its servants.

During the First World War, when records of Cabinet meetings were first kept, the first secretary of the JIC, Lord Haldane, started a book of memorable sayings by ministers. One was that of Lord Curzon, a particularly aristocratic aristocrat, during a discussion of post-war plans and procedure. Wanting to seem 'with it', he used a word he had seen but never heard spoken. He said: 'I suppose the common people will want some sort of bee-arno.' I know exactly how Haldane felt as he smothered a smile and wrote it down.

Such light relief seldom came our way. Our routine work was the task of being constantly ready to enable the JIC to formulate and issue advice about emergencies to the chiefs of staff, members of the Foreign Office or the Cabinet very quickly. The routine was such that it was a continuing rehearsal, in slower time, and within working hours of the emergency procedure. On the day before the JIC met, staff members of all the committee members' departments met in a lower-order body, the Heads of Sections. Chaired by a middle-ranking Foreign Office official, the heads would review current matters and discuss whether, and if so, how much, they mattered. Having done the same sort of thing in the Far East, I knew the risks of not detecting what was important. I was also able to use my experience of the opposite tendency – that of inflating threats, not always for reputable reasons. Deflating such untruths usually meant establishing the facts, for which, in the Far East, we asked the representative of the enormous Joint Intelligence Bureau in Melbourne (a classic example of which had been discrediting an American report of a large force of Chinese Communist heavy piston bombers threatening Singapore). The Melbourne Bureau dealt with this doctored information by pointing out that there were not enough airfields in the whole of China with runways long enough to accommodate more than the British spy-based estimate of ten. From time to time the head office in London did much the same for the JIC.

The Heads of Sections digest drafted by me and approved by the Foreign Office, who always held the whip handle of the chair, went to the JIC meeting the following day. There, John Hunt and I would be next to the chairman, by custom, another foreign official of under-secretary-ambassador rank. They looked at our review plus longer-term material written by the London Joint Intelligence Staff (JIS), grander and idler than their Far East counterparts had been in my time. When a matter came up that was within the parish of my assistants, they would creep in, ready with whispered advice, information and sometimes, most agreeably, repartee.

After the meeting came minute writing, finalized by John Hunt, who had a talent for making chaotic and inconclusive discussions look suave, rounded and ice-clear. The result would go, along with finalized studies and estimates, to the customers, usually the secretariat of the chiefs of staff in the Ministry of Defence. Typically they would use them for writing or revising contingency plans, of which there were vast numbers covering what to do and how to do it. One humble example was our very own Far East 'seizure of a beach head on the Chinese mainland' (rhythmically chiming, as I always thought with 'Quinquireme of Nineveh' from John

123

Masefield's *Cargoes*). A major project, the biggest ever, was the plan for the D-Day invasion of Europe in 1944. The range and comprehensiveness of the library of plan was such as to make it odd and perverse that such predictable adventures as the Iraq wars had been launched apparently devoid of an intelligence forecast of the aftermath and a plan for dealing with it.

The everyday fare, importing as it did knowledge of all that was going on in the intelligence world, had great intrinsic interest. But the best part of my work was people watching. Top of my personal scrapbook was the Foreign Secretary at the time, Alec Douglas-Home, later to become Prime Minister. In John Hunt's absence I was summoned to brief him on an aspect of Soviet skulduggery that had figured in a JIC report. He was at an enormous desk, which looked as if it had been there since, as the RAF saying goes, Pontius was a pilot. He listened, asked questions and thanked me. Next in my line was Sir Hugh Stevenson, JIC Chairman, liked by all of us who had known him in the Far East for his lofty detachment from the plebeian doings in Saigon, where he had been an ambassador. In one of the sheaves of telegrams that we had to sift through was a humdrum analysis from him of affairs in Vietnam ending, with ineffable true blue detachment:

> There was another explosion in the city last night but I don't yet know what it was about.

He had the high colour that would once have denoted a bottle-of-port-a-day man, and after a further ambassadorship, this time in South Africa, was said to have died of drink. But while he was with us he did an excellent job. He would certainly have seen off the poisonous attempts at playing politics with the JIC that have done great harm, as allegations about succeeding chairpersons have since shown.

His deputy, a duty performed in turn by the service members, was the Director of Military Intelligence, Major General Hugh Lloyd, whose prolix schoolmarm interventions made me put him in imaginary drag. His naval colleague was Admiral Norman Denning, who spoke seldom, but when he did he was unfailingly wise. This was not surprising because he was one of three brilliant brothers – an outstanding general, an admiral, and a judge, whom I had encountered as a law student and would meet again in the Middle Temple. His reasoning in a classic case known as 'High Trees House' was wonderfully intricate. I asked him about it when I met him in the Middle Temple in his nineties. He remembered the reasoning but had forgotten how he reached the conclusion.

One secret department representative was Sir Clive Loehnis, head of the Government Communications headquarters, the nation's eaves-droppers, usually in checks and foulards as if bound for the horse races and seemingly bored. Another was Sir Christopher Hollis, very bright but later tainted with a charge of communist leanings. The third was Sir Dick White, head of MI6, whose name was never mentioned or written other than as 'C', self-effacing and as informative and penetrating as one might have expected. The most intriguing member was Major General (retired) Sir Kenneth Strong, for many years head of JIB. He was tall, amazingly ugly and well past his best. His main accomplishment was to speak at inter-minable length off the point. At one memorable meeting he forgot that, as was the custom, representatives of the American Central Intelligence Agency (CIA) had joined us and spoke at the usual length on a topic classified as 'UK Eyes Only' and thus to be mentioned only in the earlier 'Brits only' session. No amount of fidgeting and paper rustling could staunch the flow and my JIB assistant whispered, 'Poor old Kenneth, his brush gets broader and broader.' It was with a mixture of relief and revelation when, afterwards, the head CIA man told us not to worry, the CIA, he assured us, knew about it already. That incident confirmed what I had long suspected: that the CIA was breaking a strict US-UK convention that neither would spy upon the other. So, no doubt, were we. The incident put a gloss on the CIA's custom of generous entertainment of their British opposite numbers. Rachel and I, small fry as we were, were twice dined expensively and taken to perform-ances at the Royal Opera House Covent Garden.

John Hunt and I worked well enough together and he was invariably generous with his praise. But he continued to lack warmth, notably with me and my lieutenant colonel colleague. When I discovered that he had spent the Second World War entirely in the Commonwealth Relations Office I saw why. Like others with similar background whom I had met, he felt that we thought the less of him on that score – a totally mistaken idea – and was offhand as a result. Our relationship deteriorated when, on an idle afternoon, I had taken my law books away from my noisy office to the quiet of the JIC meeting room to study. An hour or so later he burst in and stared at the books and papers on the table. On seeing that they were not, as I am sure he suspected, classified papers that I was copying, he beat an embarrassed retreat. He left soon afterwards, returning some years later to serve with great distinction as Secretary of the Cabinet.

The most significant of all was not the most senior. He was Nicholas ('Nikko') Henderson, Chairman of the Heads of Sections. He was an archetypal Foreign Office luminary – languid, debonair and able without effort to convince others of the soundness of his views. I greatly enjoyed working with and for him at his brisk and humorous meetings and even more his lightning capacity to improve my efforts to reduce the proceedings to a concise summation. I came to know him better when a slipped disc confined him to his house in Montpellier Square, where for some weeks I called to keep him up to date and receive his guidance. He went on to achieve the unique distinction of ambassadorships in all three plum posts – Moscow, Paris and, hauled back from retirement, Washington. It was a joy to run into him many years later when he opposed me in a debate in the Oxford Union, of which he had, of course, been president. He was succeeded by Edward Youde, newly returned from the embassy in Beijing, where his courage and determination in dealing with the Chinese over the detention of the Royal Navy destroyer HMS *Amethyst* in the Yellow River had enhanced his already high reputation.

As a sideline I was Secretary to the Scientific and Technical Sub-committee Standing Committee, known as STISC. Like Strubby, the airfield whose name I tried to turn into a derogatory epithet, the acronym, with its combination of 'stiff' and 'brisk', would have done as an adjective for itself. The chairman was Dr Percival Potts, learned in nuclear matters and anxious not to overstate the extent of the threats the committee dealt with and the political pressures to do so that I am sure he faced. Though still bound by the Official Secrets Act, I can say that there was nothing in any of our assessments that in any way supported the case for a British independent deterrent.

John Hunt's successor could hardly have been more different or the change more welcome. He was John Roper, a counsellor in the Foreign Office, which he had entered after service in the Scots Guards. It only emerged after his death that his exploits under cover in the Balkans had been legendary. A big, bluff man, he did not so much arrive as burst upon the scene with a porter behind him laden with expensive-looking framed paintings. These, he told us, were surplus stock from the art gallery that his wife had run in Paris. John got permission to hang the pictures in the office as replacements for the indifferent prints that had hung there hitherto. They showed to great advantage.

John was less well versed in the ways of the Civil Service than his predecessor and I enjoyed supporting him as well as his breezy company. Almost at once we were shocked by a report on the missile crisis involving President Kennedy and Secretary General Khrushchev. It began when John asked me to find out at once whether NATO had missiles in Turkey pointing at targets in the Soviet Union. My frantic calls to the Ministry of Defence confirmed that they did; and this piece of, as I imagined, the jigsaw of possible counter-action fell into place. There followed a flurry of lower-level meetings and then, on a Sunday, a JIC meeting. The three flustered CIA men, whom we did not know, briefed the committee on the now extreme confrontation, illustrating their account with satellite photographs of missiles in place in Cuba. The committee, and especially Sir Hugh, adjured the intelligence community not to drop their guard over other sources of threat that opportunists might exploit. The members left for their war dispositions, all knowing that Britain and her nuclear deterrent might well be a Soviet first-strike target. The other staff shared my view of Britain's helplessness and the potentially catastrophic risk created by the so-called independent deterrent. We also shared the minority opinion that what had been crucial in the climb-down were not nuclear weapons but the huge American conventional forces ranged against Cuba.

Meanwhile, domestic life was good. The flat was pleasant, despite its being suburban. Commuting was easy and we were within easy reach of Ardingly. However, our property, we thought, was devalued because of scruffy garages in a corner of the estate where the freeholders – property developers Freshwaters – were proposing to build yet another block of flats to add to the warren. We were desperate to prevent what we thought would wreck the estate. With gross impropriety I wrote to Freshwaters on Cabinet Office headed paper asking them to change their minds. I was at once invited to their offices in Bloomsbury by a Mr Stern, later to break the world record for the size of his bankruptcy. He convinced me with plans and drawings that what was proposed was as much for our benefit as leaseholders as it was for theirs, assuring me that it would put up the value of the entire estate. It did.

The Ropers, highly social beings, soon asked us to a dinner party in their huge rented flat in Charles Street, Mayfair. After champagne cocktail aperitifs, an excellent burgundy accompanied the sumptuous meal. The talk flowed as freely as the Volnay. How, we wondered, a counsellor (equivalent to commodore, brigadier or air commodore) could afford such an expensive dwelling soon emerged. His wife had been a Miss Roebuck, of Sears Roebuck, the giant American mail order firm. Anything they needed was flown to them by the firm, and it was her father who had bought her the art gallery in Paris. They were a knockabout couple, both hot-tempered, as their shouted telephone brawls, audible in the offices adjoining his, made embarrassingly evident. But both were charming and companionable. John eventually left the Cabinet Office for the ambassadorship in Luxembourg, regarded by the gossips as highly suitable for a gifted but lethargic man. Years later he paid me the compliment of congratulating me on my work in the peace movement.

Meanwhile, the stimulus of my job waned, as it seemed to have done for my other ground occupations. I seemed hopelessly remote from flying; and having for the first time in twenty years got out of practice, I felt the anxiety that I had occasionally felt over the years coming back. Would I, I wondered, be up to returning to high performance jets, and did I feel able to run the V bomber station I was likely to be sent to? Another element was the contempt for British nuclear weapon policy that had grown so much in the light of my JIC experience and the opinions of bright, knowledgeable colleagues. Yet another was the delight of a settled base in which our sons could flourish if only we could keep it going. We could not.

Chapter 19

Time for Benevolence

My worries about flying vanished as if by magic. I was to do a refresher flying course on the piston-engined Varsity – a type with which I was already familiar. In my past, when I had myself given refresher training to out-of-practice senior officers, I had disparagingly referred to the process as trying to turn a prune back into a plum. This was by no means apposite because the eponymous Pilot Officer Prune made, in his own way, a very useful contribution to the prevention of flying accidents. He was a fictitious figure of a pilot, accounts of whose no less fictitious antics appeared in well-produced summaries of mishaps and near misses. There were usually anonymous accounts in a section headed 'I learnt about flying from …'

Now it was my turn for refreshment and I, potentially a Pilot Officer Prune, hoped the course would prove fruitful. Thereafter I was to command a two-squadron station of Hastings four-engined transports, the oldest aircraft still in service with the RAF but capacious and versatile enough to air-drop a Land Rover. My relief at such an easy flying option was inexpressible. The station was Colerne, near Bath, a beautiful part of the West Country and even more convenient for Rachel's family home in Glastonbury. The station had been built as part of the pre-Second World War expansion scheme, opening as a group headquarters in 1940. A year later, it housed a maintenance unit and then became the base for 87 Squadron of Hurricanes, initially day and then night fighters. It got a good start when a Beaufighter, pilot unknown, shot down a Junkers Ju88 near Shepton Mallet, repeating that achievement by destroying a succession of Ju88s and Heinkel 111s.

The station had no runways until 1941. Thereafter there was a succession of fighter units. As a training base, it was equipped with Defiant night fighters and later became operational for 600 (City of London) Auxiliary Air Force Squadron. (The AAF is comparable to the Territorial Army units dating back to 1912 – the year when volunteers were re-organized. An early constituent was the field ambulance commanded by my father from 1915 until the First World War ended.) Then came another AAF squadron, 501, which had its aircraft changed from Hurricanes to Spitfires. Once they were declared operational on the Spitfire they initially flew convoy escort patrols, then went on to Rhubarbs (a code name for low-level strikes against ground targets in occupied Europe). After the Second World War, Colerne became a dumping ground for air-craft and spare parts awaiting sales. A tender form dated December 1946 shows four Avro Lancastrians (a transport conversion of the Lancaster), twenty Miles Martinet target tugs and twenty Miles Martinet trainers being put up for sale.

Six weeks' bumbling around in the Varsity, although tame and staid, was as refreshing as it was a refresher. There followed a longer course on the Hastings, which had a reputation for being difficult to fly. That I found to be so, but its main vice of swinging on landing had also been true of the Harvard. The art of prevention was the same on both: never give the swing a chance to start in the first place. I never let it happen until a year or so later at Colerne during an experience trip with David, our elder son, then an Oxford University Air Squadron cadet. Such was my flow of parental expatiation that I forgot to keep straight with the rudder. We ambled across the grass, fortunately firm, from which we were delivered ignominiously by tractor. Something biblical at the back of my mind reminded me that a prophet on his own patch may find himself without honour.

The Hastings course was at Thorney Island, the pleasant coastal station that had come in useful for school outings from nearby Ardingly. As a group captain I at first found myself being treated as a slight joke. Unlike more junior aircrew mortals, station commanders were not expected to be more than acquainted with their aircraft, a little light practice sufficing to fit them for dilettante participation in their station's flying commitments. Thorney Island's station commander was a case in point, sharpened by his habit of bunking off to Sandown Park race meetings. I would have none of that, virtuously setting about qualifying for parachutist and supply-dropping like everybody else, and as soon as I had the Hastings flying hours required, acquiring a passenger-carrying category. (Transport Command had emulated its Flying Training counterpart with an hours-plus-flying test for categorization.) To my regret, I was in such a hurry to start my new job that I decided not to try and do the three-week parachutist training course that would have enabled me to, as it were, jump to it.

RAF Colerne was run-down. Even our house-to-be lacked the improvements to which station commanders were entitled, notably an enlarged living room for guests to enjoy what the miserably small entertainment allowance partly provided for. The runways, hangars and workshops were adequate, but much needed doing for the 1,800 airmen and their families, many with their men away, on two large residential estates at nearby Pucklechurch, which were part of the Colerne bailiwick. The need was for energy and push from the top, which had not been forthcoming from my predecessor. He was a passed-over former fighter pilot who had jogged along, highly sociable, much liked and, as I suspected, with the devil-may-care insouciance that characterized some members of the fighter fraternity. He wrote letters in his own hand or, occasionally, used his secretary. I thought that odd, because he had a Dictaphone. Starting to use it myself, I checked to see whether there were any leftover bits of dictation. I was delighted to find one by an unidentifiable wag writing a spoof of Station Routine Orders:

Sport. Tennis rackets are to be returned to stores and balls to the Station Warrant Officer.

His hobby had been a land yacht in which, when there was no flying, he cruised the runways on his own, curtailing the activities of the Bannerdown Gliding Club. His other fancy, made in the workshops, was a train of trucks like those provided at seaside resorts. It carried guests, suitably fortified, from his house to the officers' mess when there were parties.

Hoping to start with a bit of éclat, I borrowed a Meteor from the Central Flying School, to be greeted on landing by a reception party, suitably impressed, I hoped, by a jet-qualified boss. My predecessor briefed me about our superiors. The group commander was Air Vice-Marshal 'Duke' Mavor. Above him, in what some saw as the 'Ogre's Castle' at Upavon, was the Commander-in-Chief, Air Marshal Sir Kenneth 'Bing' Cross. He was unpopular and much feared because of his ruthlessness and bouts of temper, contributed to perhaps by the ordeal of flying Hurricane fighters from aircraft carriers in the Second World War in a desperate attempt to conquer newly invaded Norway, during which he had flown with great bravery. Rachel and I found ourselves thrust into his company almost at once at a Bath Rugger Club ball to which the local establishment had invited us. He was as uncivil as his wife Brenda was charming. Many years later, after Bing's retirement, they bought an antique shop in London. Tragically, while she was minding it, she was murdered.

I had a mixed company under me at Colerne. The two squadron commanders were Tom Saunders and Bill Dodimead, both solid air crew operators. The chief engineer officer, Wing Commander Philip Cowmeadow, was highly qualified but had served mostly in staff posts and had about him an other-worldliness that seemed inappropriate to the eighteen elderly Hastings in his charge, and even more so to dealing with the airmen looking after them. As to the squadron aircrews, many had done little other than fly Hastings and were understandably set in their ways. Most of our overseas scheduled and special flights were routed across Europe, with high rates of cancellations and premature returns because of perceived un-flyable weather over the Massif Central on the way. I took the first chance to do a trip myself on a day when the cloud tops were forecast to exceed 20,000 feet – 2,000 feet or so above our usual operating height. My navigator, a senior old transport sweat, was clearly uneasy and his satisfaction was barely concealed when, in severe turbulence and icing cloud, hailstones shattered the plastic dome used for astro-navigation and, as my Dakota supply-dropping at Arnhem had shown, also for seeing what was happening behind – comparable perhaps to a rear-view mirror. Responding to the old sweat's bolshily professed doubts about where we were after a long time in cloud, I made use of the self-navigating pilot's friend – a radio beacon near Tripoli coded 'Romeo Oscar'. The trip, I hoped, would leaven the lump of reluctance of other old sweats and bolster the notion of a hands-on leader.

The bedrock of morale was good food and we were lucky to have a catering officer promoted from the ranks as a cook, well versed in all the wrinkles. I often visited the dining halls at meal times, occasionally donning a white overall and encouraging the giving of larger helpings. Scarcely less important was the NAAFI (Navy, Army and Air Force Institute), ready for opening after being re-furbished. I was the first bar customer, downing a pint using the old trick of a throat-opened swallow and earning points from the airmen and the local press. We gave a reopening concert, starring the singer Lulu in her earliest days, who at the time was backed by three dreadful youths called The Luvvers and escorted by a road manager. We had to pay what seemed to me an enormous fee, out of which all expenses had to be met, leaving, as he explained, very small net earnings. Later on, *The Times* music critic described Lulu, with his usual acuity, as possessed of a built-in foghorn. She has since, of course, enjoyed a long and successful career. Another musical venture that went down well, recipient of greatly increased support, was the small, struggling amateur brass band fostered by an enter-prising sergeant. It soon flourished and, by eliminating the need to import one of the RAF regional bands for ceremonial occasions, was a big plus for the station.

Raising a different kind of morale was the revival of the station gliding club, the Bannerdown, which had been largely denied its weekend freedom by the monopolizing at weekends by my predecessor's land yacht. Reviving my neglected skill as a gliding instructor, I reinforced the junior officer who had somehow kept it going, and we gradually recruited other air crews and even a few wives to have a go in our T21 trainer. Apart from the trainer we also had two Grunau Baby high performance solo models and a pilot of championship quality. The direct benefit was slight, but there in the sky was an outward and visible sign of things happening.

Less susceptible to improvement was the perennial problem of aircraft noise over Bath, unavoidable because the city lay below our circuit zone. 'Disgusted' was seldom out of the local papers, and local radio phone-ins proliferated. Explanations and a sympathetic ear at the end of a special telephone did little good. The best I could do was to invite the local MPs, Sir James Brown of Bath, Daniel Awdry of Chippenham and Paul Dean of Wiltshire, to fly round in a Hastings with me and have the problem pointed out. This they duly did, with much publicity and an excellent lunch, disposing them to accept that putting up with the noise was part repayment of the debt to the brave boys in blue.

There were soon rumblings from the Ogre's Castle, to which, like Childe Harold to the Dark Tower, I came in answer to a summons. Sir Bing was furious because, as he alleged, I had ignored his injunction to me to look after the Air Training Corps unit at his old school – Kingswood, near Bristol. Having expected and got ready for an outcry, I told him that three officers, including myself, had given the boys lectures; that they had used enough ammunition on their shooting range to meet the training needs of 120 airmen for a year; and that some 200 miles of RAF transport had been used illicitly on their behalf. Mollified, he told me to do something about our awful officers' mess.

I did. Using the talents and enthusiasm of Peter Brownjohn, a bright administrator with a flair for design, we spent the small refurbishment fund on wide timber friezes at curtain height around the walls of the public rooms, replacing the institutional green with bold and unusual colours. With new carpets and embellishments, the effect was dramatic and widely admired, not least by Sir Bing, who took to bringing small parties of his friends to supper from time to time.

I arranged for more of the funds that should have been used for maintenance to be spent on improving the churches. The Anglicans had a literal and metaphorical barn, wartime architecture at its dreary worst, and the Methodists a glorified hut. On the initiative of our vigorous and ingenious chaplain, Peter Grimwood, and his Methodist colleague, we tidied them both up. Peter found a local plastic manufacturing factory capable of large-scale works. They made us a blue fibreglass tower about 15 feet high. Welcoming the job and the attendant publicity, the helicopter squadron at Odiham collected it and lowered it onto a prepared site on the church roof. The result was a boost for the congregation and the factory, as well as a triumph for Peter and a further success at putting Colerne on the map.

The same object was served by the annual Battle of Britain open days that took place in September at bases near centres of population. Months of preparation went into welcoming the public in the largest possible numbers to watch aircraft perform (as had the Vulcan in my days as a show-off pilot) and spend money on the ground attractions. The main image-maker was the VIP enclosure, to which the Bath establishment expected invitations. Theirs was the most favoured viewing point near the control tower, part of which housed a champagne bar and buffet, paid for ostensibly by my tiny entertainment allowance and other funds from only the Lord and the accounting officer knew where. Also worth watching by us as hosts was the assembly of the grandees. One was the self-effacing Duke of Newcastle, owner of a stately home at the bottom of the hill and never known to complain of the aircraft noise that he must have suffered there. Also present was a young peer, a young man anxious to get hold of an RAF physical training instructor for what, I suspected, were philanthropic purposes, and who had difficulty in taking no for an answer. There were mayors from Bath and Bristol and the colourful chief constable of the former. He had been a sergeant pilot and had a Distinguished Flying Medal. He was given, during his frequent visits to our officers' mess for liquid refreshment, to haranguing anybody who would listen about fast-driving RAF transport on the main road into the city. Soon after raising it again with me, he was rendered apoplectic on his way home at 30mph, when our largest crane, a Coles, summoned urgently by his deputy, tore past him at its maximum speed of 50. When he saw it in use for the rescue of an injured driver stuck in his car under the railway bridge in the city centre, his mood changed from 'down with Colerne' to 'drinks all round'.

Our most picturesque grandee was Lord Long of Wraxall, an ancient widower and, as he was fond of telling anyone who would listen, grandson of the politician George Canning (1770-1827), who had teamed up with his contemporary, Viscount Castlereagh. He arrived decked out in houndstooth check and a bowler in a vintage Rolls-Royce, lording it over those he regarded as peasants. Apart from that he had great olde worlde charm and Rachel and I got to know him better. We were invited to his large run-down house in Wraxall village, a stone's throw from Colerne and staffed by one old ex-nanny-turned-housekeeper. There were signs of Baron Hardup neglect all round.

The meal, an enormous high tea, followed my taking the salute at the march past of the Royal British Legion (commanding officer, Lord Long), not unlike Captain Mainwaring and his warriors on parade. I had to shout my stirring address to the troops drawn up on the other side of a main road with traffic hurtling past. We then repaired to the village pub (in case you haven't guessed it already, The Long Arms), where he pushed the rest of the clientele aside so that the 'quality' could be served.

The combined effect of the revival and refurbishments at Colerne brought about a palpable improvement in our surroundings and morale. I had given much less time to flying than I would have liked, which was just as well because it prevented me from getting in the squadron commander's way. But I did do a representative selection of our overseas trips. I ferried many people to and from overseas postings, including Dickie Wakeford and his family, whom we had known so well, to Singapore, along the well-flown routes to the Middle and Far East. Dickie, incidentally, had a brilliant career. After the job in Kuala Lumpur, which I had been offered and had turned down, he steadily ascended, retiring as an air chief marshal and was thereafter offered the civilian job of Director General of Intelligence, which he turned down. He and his wife Ann retired to Scotland, living in the village of Fochabers, near Nairn. Ann sadly died not long afterwards and he followed her a year or two later.

My ferrying trips took me to Khormaksar airfield for what was then the colony and protectorate of Aden, site of the errant Sir Lawrence Sinclair's peccadillo, where I found myself stopping over on the day of Winston Churchill's death. That event, long planned for and kept constantly ready to implement by a one-star general specially appointed for the task, was codenamed 'Hope Not', expressing every incumbent's desire that it would not happen on his watch. The plan drew on almost every service in the UK, Colerne's quota being the four smart airmen whom we had earmarked. After the death there was the usual flood of mawkish lament in the media. One exception that appealed to me came, surprisingly, from the *Daily Mail*, then, as now, not known for its literary merit:

> *So faded a summer cloud away,*
> *So stills the wind when storm is o'er,*
> *So gently shuts the eye of day*
> *The rest is come*

I never did discover who the author was. Most of us with wartime recollections of Churchillian leadership recall a specific speech. At a terribly dangerous stage of my time in the bomber business, I appreciated his tribute to bomber crews, uttered to complement his 'Never in the course of human history has so much been given to so many by so few.' It was:

Unwearied by their constant challenge and mortal danger, our bomber pilots attack targets deep in enemy territory with relentless zeal, night after night.

Not true, but sustaining. I was glad not to be sucked into the obsequies.

Returning from other overseas trips, I was irked, as were all the Colerne crews, at having to land at nearby Lyneham for customs clearance. The station commander there was Group Captain Alasdair Steedman. We had served together as instructors at Cranwell and directing staff at the Joint Services Staff College, the latter having been the scene of the different approaches to an exercise that I have already reported. He poured good-tempered scorn on the grubby old Hastings that sullied his immaculate tarmac apron, meant mainly for the Shiny Ships, as the new Britannia propeller-jet transports based at his station were called. The Hastings differed from Bad Bear's idleness at Latimer only in that it was incontinent of the engine oil that did the sullying. That was not the only affliction suffered by our ancient aircraft. We began trips more or less fully serviceable, our ancient aircraft collecting snags en route. The hope was that they would remain minor enough to let us finish our trips. Our longest scheduled service, for the small Army detachment still based at Belize in what was still British Honduras, involved servicing by the USAF, who called us 'the Flintstones'. All of this enabled me to put a case, fought for months and in the end successful, for customs facilities of our own at Colerne. In a flash, most of our serviceability problems seemed to evaporate, along with the nugatory and highly undesirable process known as Christmas Treeing. It was a robbing-Peter-to-pay-Paul practice, nugatory in that serviceability in the long run got worse.

Suddenly, in June 1965, tragedy struck the busy, prosperous and happy station that I and a lot of other devoted people had struggled to create. A Hastings, full of trainee parachutists who were about to do practice jumps near the neighbouring base at Abingdon, nosedived into the ground. All aboard were killed. By far the worst aspect was of course the human tragedy, and my colleague, the Abingdon station commander, had to bear the worst consequences such as dealing with the bodies, clearing the wreckage and a deluge of admin. We, however, had our share and the first job was to tell the families. Collecting Rachel and the chaplain, Peter Grimwood, I toured the married quarters of all who were based at or near Colerne breaking the news. All the wives accepted it with the most moving dignity and calm. For all the stricken families there was massive and immediate support from the close community of RAF neighbours. Rachel did her job magnificently, helping one young wife, who was feeding the baby, by letting her family know and asking them to come to her.

The funeral procession at Abingdon was headed by the station commander and me flanking Sir Bing. All three of us had our best blue uniforms deluged in the pouring rain and were pleasantly surprised that the air blue barathea, to give it its proper name, dried out undamaged.

The vital job of discovering the cause was soon done. It was the failure, through metal fatigue, of two of the four bolts that held the elevators. Hastings aircraft throughout the RAF, few of which were not at Colerne, were grounded and given a 'retro-fit' with much stronger bolts. Implementing it on all aircraft would take months. Even as we completed our own share of the funerals and burials in Colerne village churchyard, I recognized the imminent morale problems that would arise on a flying station that could not fly.

The problems were not insuperable. The air crews were sent on initiative exercises to see who could get the furthest without having to pay for transport: one enterprising young man finished up in South America. There was much make-do-and-mend to be done and the sub-inspections preceding Duke Mavor's second and inevitably meticulous inspection were looming. The small initial training unit for would-be RAF Regiment parachutists carried on. I could give more attention to the detached family housing sites under my jurisdiction, coming across on an inspection a phenomenon not seen before even by the highly experienced maintenance staff: one problem family, bereft of fuel and having squandered their welfare payments, had sawn up the stairs, which they used for fuel to keep warm by keeping a fire going on the ground floor of their house. Highly amusing, I reflected, but indicative of a failure on the part of the RAF in its duty to instil discipline, honesty and common sense into the airman whose family had been stupid and destructive.

Another diversion gave me a glimpse of how useful my slowly growing grasp of criminal law might come in. A flight engineer officer asked of his batwoman a service well outside the normal run – a sexual favour. Such was the girl's embarrassment when, with her mother present, I asked her what had happened she could only bring herself to describe the object of her attentions as 'his carrot'. I told her that, if she went to court, her evidence would have to include detailed anatomical and physiological descriptions of what she saw and did. She would, I explained, also have her own sex life minutely investigated and exposed during cross-examination and would be accused of provocation, known in the vernacular as 'asking for it'. I assured her that I had powers (under Queen's Regulation 1154, as it then was) tough enough to deter any repetition and diminish her abuser's chances of promotion and would use them to the full. She decided not to proceed. I kept a useful officer and saved much adverse publicity. But I also found myself on the horns of a dilemma when the offender's wife, having got wind of what had happened, came to our house hoping I would tell her more. Doing my best not to spoil the marriage, I told her I had dealt with the matter and the best thing to do was to forgive and forget. This, it seemed, is what she did.

From the flying standpoint I was one of the lucky ones, using my instructing skill not only with the gliding club but also with cadets in the station Chipmunk, which worked overtime with refresher, experience and training flights. The cadets included our two sons, respectively taught elementary flying in the Oxford University Air Squadron Chipmunks and the RAF cadetship scheme school near Andover in the Jackaroo, a Tiger Moth fitted with a canopy. The small museum of aircraft originated with the last station commander but one got a major brush-up and I added to its complement by collecting a time-expired Valetta from Kemble. Even more welcome would have been a Viking, its civil version.

There were no idle hands for Satan to find work for and, all in all, spirits remained high. In a reply to a signal to all stations in the group asking for the useless information that seemed so important to the staff, I ended with: 'Our tails may be off but they're still up, earning, I gathered, approbation from Messrs Duke and Bing.

The technical outcome of the accident did not reflect well on the chief technical officer. He had, it emerged, failed to act on a file note by a junior engineer officer recommending a check on the very bolts that had failed. He had caused me concern from the first, and I was relieved when the tortuous procedure I had initiated months earlier finally worked. It was a complicated process, not necessarily discrediting the officer concerned. It did not indicate anything adverse. It simply meant that I was sure he would serve more effectively in a different post. In due course he returned to the staff work in which he excelled. I sympathized with him over the domestic fallout of another move and a break in the continuity of his children's' education. He was replaced by a tough, engaging Welsh ex-airman whose rise to wing commander had happened mostly on stations and who knew everything about the Hastings.

The awful non-flying hiatus ended when I tested the first retrofitted aircraft. The same local press and radio that had made such a fuss about aircraft noise rose to the bait of a seemingly risky flight, in reality no more dangerous than any other bit of aviation. As we all got under way again I had another piece of luck. One of our fuel-testing airmen discovered a small shortfall in the calorific value in a consignment of fuel from Esso. The defect created a theoretical risk because the consequence would be a reduction in the range of aircraft using the fuel (though in reality the obligatory safety margins we always provided would have absorbed the deficiency). The Esso representative, anxious not to lose the supply contract to Shell, called to apologize and, over lunch, asked me to suggest a way in which Esso could express their regret. I at once mentioned the station commander's ceremonial sword, used for AOC inspections and whenever we exercised our right as Freemen to march through Bath. The sword had to be borrowed from a central store of less than immaculate weaponry. Perhaps Esso, I suggested, would care to give us one of our own. Within a day or so I went to the Wilkinson Sword Company in London – no doubt the stock was periodically replenished with ploughshares for beating – to get one fitted. It became the station's pride and joy and still rests in the huge stock of squadron silver kept in a hangar along with other presentation swords, silver models of aircraft donated by generous members of the squadrons equipped with them, and doubtless other clobber. Some of the models, still to be seen in the RAF Club in London, are works of art.

There followed a personal plus. I had a letter from Sir Bing asking me to try to recruit from the 300 or so young aircrew on the station more members for the RAF Club, at that time in decline. That such a request from such a source was necessary indicated anxiety on high but was not surprising. The building in Piccadilly had been presented as a thank you offering to the RAF in 1922 by Lord ('Bearno') Curzon. I had been invited there by a member some years earlier and was so unfavourably impressed that I decided that the club was not for me. Apart from the silver models there was nothing to commend and much to deplore. Copies of the daily papers were pinned up inconveniently on easels and seedy members, accepted Heaven knows how, tried to flog insurance policies – especially the ones covering death, which, for aircrew involved high premiums and fat commissions. In any event, a generous uncle had given me a membership at his own club, the Junior United Services.

The problem of recruiting members from Colerne was forbidding. That was because the sole aim in life for many of our air crews was to get lucrative jobs in the aviator-starved world of civil airlines. I was not optimistic. However, after months of pleading, cajoling and threatening we had achieved what I thought was a derisory result. My devoted henchman, Wing Commander John Tipton, chief administrator and navigator by trade, with a mathematical bent, did a sum. He remarked that neither he nor I were members and if we both joined the Colerne club percentage would rise by a few second places of decimals. That we did and I sent a tremulous reply. To our surprise, Sir Bing congratulated me on doing well on a very difficult wicket.

Recruitment of members of the club remains a perennial problem, eased by concessions such as reduced subscription rates for junior officers and, for elderly members, freedom from the unavoidable increases that have to be imposed from time to time. Successive chairmen (usually, air vice-marshals stationed at the Ministry of Defence) have presided over the network of committees and volunteers. The result has been a steady succession of improvements to facilities such as extra bedrooms, better catering and a variety of refurbishments. The public rooms are much in demand for wedding receptions, private dinners and cocktail parties. The demand is such that dates are best booked upwards of a year ahead – a precaution I have taken for the many parties that have been signposts in our family's history. All in all, the club's record is a story of success.

Sir Bing's effort, doubtless part of a high-level initiative on the part of the powers that were, had borne fruit and he thanked me profusely for the little I had done – very different in manner from his habitual grumpiness. Indeed, he was effusively civil when we said goodbye. I thanked him in return for his part in getting me promoted to air commodore. No less civil, he replied that I had, in effect, promoted myself.

Leaving Colerne on promotion to air commodore ended a flying career of twenty-five years, 5,000 flying hours and forty-five different kinds of aircraft. What enormous fun it had been.

Chapter 20

At Odds with Whitehall

I managed to scotch air crew opinion at RAF Thorney Island that flying group captains were a bit of a joke. I had done my best to change that opinion, flying at Colerne as productively as the rest of the job of commanding a station had allowed. Air commodores were not obliged to keep in flying practice and, with one or two exceptions, did not do so. Air vice-marshals, incidentally, were deemed to be above such a trivial pursuit. The single instance I encountered was an air commodore as big a show-off as I am who, out of bravado or in pursuit of points, had undertaken to ferry a Vampire to Africa following much the same route as I had during my CFS days. It was apparent from his signs of nervousness that he regretted the decision. Happily, all went well – a tribute to whoever had given him refresher flying training. I dreaded becoming an airborne wrinkly and thought it best not to bother and face the fact that I was once again a Whitehall warrior. There was little risk of losing another bowler because Gieves had made the expensive one I sported to fit my head. When, thirty-four years later, I took it back to them for re-blocking and overhaul, they showed me the measuring machine they had used, now in their museum. The hat spends its declining years as an adornment at peace movement marches and veterans' commemorative parades.

We had to hasten from our comfortable house at Colerne to make way for my successor, a newly promoted group captain delighted with the thriving state of the station he was inheriting. Fortunately my new job carried with it the right to a quarter and ours was a senior officers' model at Bushey, near Fighter Command head-quarters at Bentley Priory. The saving grace was an adjacent golf course, trespassing on which offered a semblance of country walks in the suburban wasteland. Behind our house lay a semi-circular tier of other houses on rising ground. Passing our back windows was like appearing in an amphitheatre. Taking Rachel's breakfast up in the morning I could feel beady eyes on me, so much so that I was tempted from time to time to play to the gallery with a commentary to go with the performance.

We were thankful when we moved to a smaller but more private house at Hendon, the most famous, perhaps, of all RAF stations and the home of the annual RAF flying display, precursor to its counterpart at Farnborough. Our sons were glad of its proximity to central London and our elder boy, David, an assiduous reader of the papers, found a job advertisement that was eventually to lead to my civilian career.

Hendon had been a familiar destination during my Dakota days. Built to accommodate the primitive biplanes, it was unpleasantly, if not dangerously, small for modern aircraft, as I knew when I landed there on the morning of the day Rachel and I were to be married and on another occasion when I delivered senior officer members of an 'establishments' committee who travelled about deciding how RAF units were to be staffed. Hendon's small size also made taking off troublesome: to get as much air space as possible one had to start right at the airfield boundary and wait until the railway line close to the opposite boundary was train-free. The station is now closed for flying, but hangars, a parachute storage and repair building, and a handsome officers' mess remain. So also does the shed housing the RAF and the Bomber Command museums. The latter had no public funding and ran into problems after overspending on exhibits to such an extent that it had to be helped out by retired officers working as fund-raisers. Both are complemented by an assembly of aircraft at Duxford and competed with by private collections such as the Shuttleworth.

The tube station for commuting to central London was Colindale and the trains were infrequent. The difficulties showed acutely on my first morning when a young lady of apparently limited literary attainment doggedly occupied the booking office window, slowly scrawling a cheque for a season ticket renewal as the queue behind her grew longer and the train, one of the few and infrequent callers at Colindale, drew out. My journey, when it at last began, was along the ghastly Northern Line and the destination, Westminster, the nearest Underground station to Whitehall.

The Ministry of Defence, an amalgam of the former Admiralty, War Office and Air Ministry, was housed in half of a huge office block between Whitehall and the Thames Embankment. Cuckoo-like, it had soon ousted what was then the Board of Trade from the other half, gaining a northern entrance dominated by stone statuary of obese female nudes. MOD (RAF), the ugly acronym for the old Air Ministry, was my workplace.

It wasn't quite a case of 'Abandon hope all ye who enter here,' but the building was foreboding. Years later it was to be the scene of a boorish refusal of admission by an official flunkey when David Ennals, a former health minister and a friend, had asked me to accompany him at an interview with Michael Heseltine. Character-istically, he made it a condition that he would be alone. Also in character, David would have none of it.

Denizens of the MOD were segregated in ascending order of grandeur. Being an acolyte of the Chief of Air Staff (CAS) put me on the fifth of the seven, in a niche of an office overlooking the row of handsome Georgian houses in Richmond Terrace, overshadowed by newer monstrosities and later replaced by an arty office block that was part of the Department of Health's Topsy-like growth. Inter-spersed was a stretch of tarmac for parking the cars of the mighty, including, at the time, the CAS's official car, appropriately numbered AM1. It also came in useful as space for parades for visiting foreign potentates – a function that involved a welcome by one or more chiefs of staff. I pitied the CAS, frequently required to change into uniform, go on parade and change back into the lounge suits we all

149

routinely wore. As the need for security increased, the hitherto open space acquired barriers and guards.

At a right-angle to the MOD building was Whitehall – source of the disparaging nickname 'Whitehall warrior' for those of us separated from normal uniformed service. In the middle of that fine street was the Cenotaph, years later the scene of CND protests and leafleting in which, as a member of ex-services CND, I took part. An eminent architect colleague told me that the memorial was so designed that its slightly sloping sides would meet at a point 1,000 feet from the ground. He didn't explain the symbolism, if any there was. Opposite my office was No. 10 Downing Street, as yet lacking the formidable barriers and gates that the paparazzi and would-be petitioners had to pass to get to the door. Thus there was plenty to look at during idle moments that were to turn out sometimes to be hours.

My job was labelled Director of Air Staff Briefing (DASB). The directorship originated early in the Second World War, when the Chief of Air Staff found his work impeded by too much advice from too many people. He appointed a brilliant young barrister, Leslie Scarman, who had left his chambers to join the RAF Volunteer Reserve. His job was to dredge and pan all that the air staff submitted, gloss it as necessary with his own comments and submit it in a concise and palatable form. Scarman, soon promoted and appointed as personal staff officer to Lord Tedder, began a long succession of DASBs. Years later, in 1968, Scarman was one of three senior lawyers who interviewed me, along with many other applicants, for the job of Under-Treasurer of the Middle Temple, of which in due course I became the latest. Later still, Scarman, having risen in his profession by way of head of chambers to the Bench, was commissioned by the government to study and report on inner-city problems in London.

Rank (in both senses) inflation had happened in the Ministry of Defence over the years but the job was the same. There was now a whole department of the Chief of Air Staff with an air marshal vice chief, three air vice marshal assistant chiefs and a bevy of air commodore directors down below, with assorted civil and service staff as back-up. There was also a deputy chief of air staff; at the time a remarkably handsome air marshal, apart from having apparently helped himself too liberally to cream cakes. Other than a personal staff officer and a secretary, he seemed to have no supporting 'lowerarchy'. Neither I nor anyone I came across knew what he did; but everybody agreed that it was not a lot.

I, too, was amply endowed with people: a group captain deputy, two wing commanders (one the son of Air Chief Marshal Sir John Slessor who had inherited his many qualities), and a retired squadron leader who had become a civil servant, the senior of two grades. These very useful people were wonderful at finding the obscure background information often needed for my briefs. I also had a knowledgeable woman secretary who knew the ropes well, enveloped semi-permanently in a cloud of cigarette smoke. On his last day in the office before he retired, the CAS at the time invited me back to the MOD to wish him well. Permeating rather than complementing the Ministry's service structure was a network of civil servants with a *Yes Minister's* Sir Humphrey lookalike at the top as Permanent Secretary, running the Ministry on behalf of all three services. Below him were deputy secretaries, under secretaries and assistant under secretaries, the last being segregated into single services. I was pleased to discover that at least one of the deputies was well disposed and had a life outside the confines of the Ministry, playing the harpsichords that he had restored. On the other hand, he could be awkward: he refused to act as a referee on my behalf when I applied for a job. He had a first-class brain that took him to permanent secretary level within a year or two.

Our segregated single-service assistant (Aus-Air, Australian Air Charterers Pty Ltd). He also had a first-class brain, which took him to permanent secretary level within a year or two, but was soon to be succeeded by the all too common has-beens that were shunted around the Civil Service until some muggins department got saddled with them. Most of the civil side, however, was remarkably capable and responsive. One striking rise to the occasion was the funding crisis in 1967–68, when the Cabinet suddenly decreed enormous reductions in expenditure – another all too common occurrence, as succeeding generations of battlers for Defence funding will testify. Voluminous excellent papers on how to set about it appeared within days. The military planners, perennially encumbered with inter-service brawls and the ponderous chiefs of staff machinery, lumbered along behind. I knew from my time in the intelligence world and as DASB what that burden of delay involved. The papers still took ages to reach the stage of chiefs of staff authority for them to be 'authorized for use in planning'.

Presiding over the MOD Colossus were the politicians. At their head was the Secretary of State, a Cabinet post notorious for the rate at which its incumbents changed. An outstanding exception was Denis Healey. The other twenty or so politicians appointed between 1945 and 1966 were a mixed bunch. None of them stayed as long as two years – just as well in some instances. A lesser light was Tom King MP, who never got to first base in understanding defence issues. That was evident from his performance in the Oxford Union, where I opposed him in a debate about nuclear weapons. Straight-laced, short-fused and poorly briefed, he reacted badly to the students' acceptance of what I blush to describe as the convincing case against Britain's so-called nuclear deterrent. He later got a job investigating breaches in security, which seemed to suit him.

Two of the other incumbents stand out from the otherwise in-different politicians that have served in the Ministry of Defence. David Owen (later Lord) realized that the Ministry was running the politicians, not the other way round, conducting an:

> insidious process of military indoctrination, the heady mixture of pomp and secrecy to which most politicians are susceptible [which] tends to blunt one's normal sensitivity.

> (Owen, *The Politics of Defence*, Jonathan Cape 1992)

Not that Owen had much sensitivity to blunt, as I was to discover years later when I encountered him as Minister of Health. A Tory predecessor, Sir John Nott, in a rare burst of getting it right in *The Times* of 10 October 1987, described the Ministry as:

a huge super tanker, well captained and engineered, the systems continually updated – but with no one ever asking where the hell it's going.

The one exception in terms of time served in office and trouble taken was the aforementioned Dennis, later to become Lord, Healey. I met him twice during my tour, while traversing the endless stretches of Ministry corridors. On both occasions he asked, apparently with genuine interest, what I did and passed the time of day. It was not until years afterwards when we were both members of a think-tank called the British American Security Information Council, that I appreciated the combination of ability and geniality that made him so outstanding a minister. Like many staff members lucky enough to receive them, I benefited from his occasional series of personally drafted and beautifully crafted minutes on difficult issues. As DASB, I found them particularly useful as pabulum for my briefs.

The latter were for my working boss, the Chief of Air Staff, Air Chief Marshal Sir Charles Elworthy, known to all as Sam. Universally popular, full of humour and possessed of a penetrating wit, he was a pleasure to work for. When I briefed him, usually with a bundle of paper, he would cross-examine me on, and often run circles round, my arguments; not surprisingly in view of his training as a barrister. He was always tolerant and amusing, even volunteering sometimes that he benefited from our talks. He was at his best at smaller meetings. He sometimes used a remarkable talent for mimicry on ministers encountered at Cabinet Defence Committee meetings attended by the chiefs of staff (only occasioned either by the chiefs' request or by the committee itself – both when military exigency necessitated consultations).

I felt I was of some help in getting him ready for the adversarial proceedings of the chiefs of staff with points that he could make in putting the RAF case. But from time to time he had to miss these preparatory sessions, change into uniform and join the ceremonial reception parade on the tarmac five floors below my office. When that happened, as my spies reported, he managed just as well, which I found a bit galling. I was sorry to see him go, promoted to the now abolished rank of Marshal of the RAF and made Chief of Defence Staff. As such he presided over a new hierarchy supposed to mediate between the conflicting service interests and formulate an agreed view. Responsibility for briefing him passed to Neil Cameron, an air commodore on the central staff. Neil spent much time learning from the single-service briefers and did his job superbly. He feared that joining the Central Staff would jeopardize his career but he could not have been more wrong. He rose meteorically to become Chief of Air Staff, retiring to become head of King's College, part of London University; of which, incidentally, I was an external student. Tragically, he died prematurely of cancer.

Below Elworthy, my administrative boss was the Vice-Chief of Air Staff (not to be confused with the sinecure Deputy Chief already mentioned) Air Marshal Sir Brian Burnett, who died aged 98 in 2011. He had recently succeeded Sir Peter Fletcher, another lawyer whom I had visited at an advanced flying school from CFS years earlier. As VCAS he had been chief protagonist in a years-long internecine battle with the Navy, the closing phases of which Burnett had inherited. The issue was whether British defence interests, in particular mounting offensives at long range, should be met by carrier-borne aircraft or from land bases in allied territories. It involved personality clashes with advocates on both sides. Doing my best to prepare our representatives epitomized all that I most disliked about my work. I was being used to do the very opposite of what the JSSC at Latimer stood for and taught: to push the RAF interest and do the Navy down.

Burnett was no Fletcher. His office was always full of files, on the enclosures of which he wrote comments in very small pencil manuscript, presumably to get counter-comments or trigger action. I seldom read them; nor, I suspect, did anybody else. He held a weekly, hard to justify meeting of selected air commodore directors with the Assistant Chief of Air Staff (Policy) and me in attendance. It was ostensibly a review of current business, but actually it consisted of subtle turf wars and self-advertisement by the directors. I was supposed to glean material for my briefs and to purvey titbits from the Chiefs of Staff Secretariat and other joint gossip centres for RAF staff. I hope I scattered as much as I gleaned, the latter process being made much more difficult by one air commodore who shall be nameless. He was so jealous of his colleagues and anxious to defend his territory that particulars of Coastal Command problems and activities had to be left out of my briefs. In striking contrast were similar meetings held occasionally by Elworthy himself. He was adept at using his barrister-like acuity to put people on their mettle. (Also adept in her way is his daughter, Scilla Elworthy, now Mrs Mclean. She is currently Director of the Oxford Research Group, with a succession of publications to her credit. Her book *In the Dark* (1989) exposes some of the skulduggery of NATO and the problems of the age of nuclear weapons. It is also an excellent source book for peaceniks like me.)

I used my forensic skill, such as it was, to help with the battle. The RAF case was weak, our prospects for creating an effective strike force having been ruined by the cancellation of the world-leading bomber/reconnaissance aircraft, the TSR2. Our main argument, repeated in numerous presentations, was that the TSR2 substitute, the Buccaneer, could provide all necessary long-range support needed for the whole gamut of contingency operations, including our obligations as a NATO power. Admittedly, Britain had to have overseas bases, but these were readily available on our own, Commonwealth, American or other allied territory. The only gap was in the Indian Ocean and to close it Britain intended to develop garrison rights on the island of Aldabra, virtually uninhabited and a treasury of wildlife. Negotiations with the Treasury and overseas departments rumbled on.

The Navy staff were withering in their scorn as British influence waned and friendly territory shrank. The Buccaneer made matters worse when it proved to be lacking in the performance claimed for it. The case for aircraft carriers, which included air defence and minesweeping and anti-submarine ships, was that they were almost impregnable. The two groups envisaged, ran the argument, could deal with any contingency. And did not the enormous US Navy, planned to have ten carrier groups, offer proof of their viability and indestructibility? No, replied the RAF, with murmurs of Pearl Harbor and Hiroshima; and what about the enormously higher construction and maintenance costs of a carrier group? The disputations, alas, have been made out of date and irrelevant. Soon after the turn of the century, much lobbying led to a decision to scrap the *Ark Royal* and build two new carriers. At the end of their very long lead time and huge cost it emerged first that the order for two would have to be reduced to one; and the news that the American-built joint strike fighters wouldn't be ready until long after the carriers were ready for service. To cap it all, one carrier would have to be laid up as soon as it was finished.

I joined the fray towards its end. I am as certain as I can be that there was no exaggeration by the naval protagonists of carriers' capabilities, just as there wasn't any misrepresentation by the RAF. The Navy, however, tended towards emotion-loaded excess of zeal. I remembered the choleric commander in charge of flying at Lossiemouth. I experienced the heat with which the cantankerous Admiral Sir Caspar John (son of the artist Augustus John) put the naval case to the Chiefs of Staff Committee. 'My Service right or wrong' seemed to me, as a mere contract man doing the job because of the free flying it offered, as blinkered a way of thinking as the dreadful nationalistic shibboleth (NEH492):

> *I vow to thee my country*
> *All earthly things above,*
> *Entire and whole and perfect*
> *The service of my love.*

Whatever the truth, the whole time-consuming and idiotic inter-necine war ended, for the time being, in a draw. We got the bases, to my relief not with Aldabra and its plethora of wildlife, but with a right of use of the USAF base at nearby Diego Garcia, already so heavily populated that our arrival made the wildlife problem no worse. The Navy kept their carriers; and later, the country was saddled with the enormous cost of replacing them, with delivery well into the twenty-first century. Before the replacement order could be more than half completed, part of it was cancelled, and, to pile on the agony, one carrier (HMS *Ark Royal*) was laid up. All part of the politicians' habit of almost indiscriminate cutting of all three services when mismanagement of the economy makes that exigent.

I was glad to be rid of my part of the whole silly business and turn to other work. This involved consulting the assistant chiefs for operations and, occasionally, operational requirements, though the latter worked so far into the future and forecasting rather than decision making that I seldom had to bother him. Running day-to-day operations was Air-Vice Marshal Bob Hodges – as bright, popular and helpful as Duke Mavor. He was later to ascend and join the elite company of presidents of the RAF Club – a demanding addition to their normal work. In return they had their portraits painted and hung on the walls of the public rooms. Within the air vice-marshals' stockade were the directors, mostly air commodores but with group captains for the lesser tasks. They varied. At one extreme were those only too anxious to use me as a conduit for impressing the all-highest. At the other were those trying to keep me at arm's length, apprehensive of thunder-theft. In the middle were the sensible and honest, who helped me to make the briefs as accurate and helpful as possible. With one of special bombast I had such trouble getting what the CAS needed to know that I feared, as we exchanged vitriolic minutes, that duelling might result.

For my wide range of contacts I could help with foreknowledge of impending horrors. The most memorable was when a storm of the economy cuts to defence funding threatened the famous Red Arrow formation aerobatic team, a hugely popular feature of many displays and universally acknowledged to be an asset to recruitment. My advance warning almost certainly saved the day: the proposal was strangled at birth.

Such achievements were rare. As I learned more of the huge apparatus of the Ministry and the extraordinary difficulties of being any use I became despondent. And as the work of preparation and brief writing became more familiar it took up less of my time and interest. I had, moreover, as an exceptionally bright deputy director, Group Captain John Nicholls, who had been a great help as I learnt the ropes but seemed as frustrated as I was at the lack of an outlet for his abilities. I fretted; but he sublimated his discontent with cheerful cynicism. He was soon posted to command a station, eventually rising high. His successor was the worst instance of a square peg in a round hole I ever came across. Pleasant and willing, he seemed to have passed through the staff college without touching the sides. He could scarcely put one word in front of another; and his inability to comprehend what was expected of him made him next to impossible to train. His presence was an advantage in that it gave the two wing commanders (one the son of Air Chief Marshal Sir John Slessor) working for him more to bite on, and me a chance to add some of what Nicholls had done to my own work. But for my successor's sake he had to go; I started the long and tortuous process of getting him moved on.

Just as boredom was really beginning to bite, I found relief in an extended outing. The Chief of Air Staff undertook periodical visits to overseas RAF units. This time he delegated the job to Duke Mavor, with me to back him up. We embarked on the eastward route, over familiar to me, in the glamorous VC10 four-engined jet transport newly in service, later to become almost the opposite as a tanker for flight refuelling. It was wonderfully smooth and comfortable but it broke down at our first stop – Malta. We continued in a Britannia, a successor to the Hastings and, in its trooping mode, almost as uncomfortable. We dropped in at Oman, Sri Lanka, Singapore and Hong Kong, over-entertained at each stop by the resident commanders.

I was fascinated to discern just the devices I had used as an airman in comparable circumstances to paper over defects and make modest achievements look impressive. A classic lowly instance, I recalled, had been in the tin room at Cardington. The airmen, finding insuperable the task of making piles of dirty meat tins and mounds of amazing grease look tidy, kept a stone on the floor that looked exactly like a potato. When inspecting officers, always young, inexperienced and gullible, told them to pick it up they would reveal that it was a door stop. There would be merry laughs all round as they ushered the greenhorn out into the wash-up next door. Of such was the account of his stewardship of RAF Hong Kong, Air Commodore North Lewis. In place of a potato stone he handed out Chinese extending pointers for use at presentations. Mine came in useful for many years, especially for talks to CND meetings and assorted didactic occasions.

Inexperienced and gullible, I was stupid enough to try and finish the duty-free gin we had bought to return the hospitality of some of our hosts. Few guests turned up, which resulted in near fatal results for the hung-over hosts. I really meant, and have kept to, my 'never again'.

Back home I had two delightful surprises. I had been awarded a CBE (Commandership of the Order of the British Empire). There was no citation, but it was safe to assume that it had to do with keeping Colerne in the best fettle I could manage. I felt sorry for my colleague station commander at Abingdon, who had had to deal with the horrifying results of the Hastings crash and had done just as good a job as I had. Rachel and both of our boys came to the investiture. This time there was no repetition of the two in one featuring my father and myself. But the queen, God bless her, managed a nod and a smile.

Almost as delightful in a different context was finding that I had passed the intermediate exams that I had taken earlier in the year for my London University LLB degree in all four subjects – Crime, Contract, Constitutional and Roman Law. Constitutional Law was the most interesting to study and I would have liked to use such Latin as I knew to delve more deeply into Roman Law. The results were posted in the Senate House in Russell Square by candidate numbers only; it took three visits to the notice board before I accepted the success was real. Such is *folie de doute*. I hastened to the Design Centre in the Haymarket to share the good news with Rachel.

Both events were encouraging, but their effect didn't last. Boredom, frustration and perhaps the absence of flying made me depressed enough to need help; but I was scared of going to MOD doctors, of whose confidence I could not be sure. I discovered that the head of St Andrew's private hospital in Northampton, where my mother had been looked after until she died, did private psychiatric practice in Harley Street. His hospital post, incidentally, was one that my father had applied for without success. He prescribed an anti-depressant that made me too drowsy to cope with my work. But his second attempt worked and in a few weeks I recovered. Years afterwards I had another attack of anxiety and depression. My excellent GP tried a number of drugs. One, at Christmas time, didn't work, but it provided a seasonal pun:

Ding Dong Merelil on High.

The drug that did work was Seroxat, aka Paroxetine, frowned upon because of its habit-forming effect. Patients, me included, usually don't let that bother them. What matters is that it works, as it has for me for many years, keeping a totally awful affliction at bay.

My recovery was given a boost when I heard on my DASB grapevine of a block of flats built in London by the MOD for those whose duties made quick access to Whitehall essential. Shamelessly, I represented my work, virtually part-time and totally devoid of urgency, as needing such access. Rachel and the boys were delighted because the block was in Ladbroke Square, near Notting Hill, regarded by youthful cognoscenti as 'with it'. Being entirely without it, I missed Hendon's squash courts and the walks over the idle airfield (now covered in housing). But I enjoyed the square's communal garden and welcomed the easy commuting.

With time on my hands I spent more of my half-filled working week with my head in my law books. Having passed the intermediate exams, I thought increasingly of the prospects that passing the final might open up. At the same time, even the bits of work not connected with the sea/air battle became ever more contentious between the services and with the civil servants. As a music hall ditty said of the soldiers:

> They're not there
> To fight the foe
> You might think so
> But oh dear no.

Instead they fought each other, giving a new meaning to the expression 'Whitehall warrior', in which, of course, I was a private. Arrogantly, as I now see, I saw my job as a waste of the talents that a favourite parable of mine enjoins us to conserve:

> *Nature findeth ample work*
> *For idle hands to do.*

I was not alone. On the adjoining perch was Air Commodore Angus Nicholson, a friend and former staff officer at 1 Group. He too lacked enough to do; and with longer experience of the MOD and greater familiarity with staff work than mine, was even more contemptuous of the overstaffed and ponderous system. Another good brain bursting to get out as soon as he could afford it was Air Commodore Micky Mount, a qualified solicitor. Yet another was Air Commodore Miller, like all his namesakes, known as 'Dusty'. He was an astute accountant who spent much of his working time making out whole books of cheques, all of which he used to apply for multiple allocations of the many new share issues launched into the stock market at the time. When their prices rose, he would sell.

My required reading expanded into more and more job advertisements. I soon tried for the post of Director of the National Association for the Care and Rehabilitation of Offenders. It failed, but the application was good experience. My next target was chief officer of the Welfare Department of the London County Council, as it then was. A very old friend who had taught me at Charterhouse and had risen in the Church to be Suffragan Bishop of Whitby, weighed in with:

> First-class ability, extremely thorough and energetic in all that he does ... will do the job really well ... lively personal interest in the people and ... situations that come his way ...

... the vacuity of which made me realize how little there was to be said for me.

161

As my ferment frothed, Sam Elworthy was succeeded by Air Chief Marshal Sir John Grandy, who had an outstanding record as a Battle of Britain pilot and had had a succession of highly successful commands. He was charming and good-hearted. Staff work, however, was not his métier. He hated having to read his way into topics and was not good at conducting problem-solving sessions. I carried on much as I had with Sam, but I doubted whether he read my briefs, or indeed much of the other paper that passed across his desk. The other chiefs of staff clearly liked him, but he carried little weight. He must have been a burden for his excellent young Civil Service private secretary, Michael Quinlan, who rose to become Permanent Secretary of the MOD. Like Nikko Henderson, I met Michael, by then Sir, again, years afterwards. Once a loyal defender of the so-called British nuclear capability, he later concluded that, had he been able to play his part in bringing it into being again, he would not have been in favour.

Chapter 21

Out of the Blue Barathea

The gloom continued. Co-incident with the change of CAS was the implementation of the 1968 cuts that the civil servants had forecast and planned. At a vice chief's meeting to consider the implications, Burnett, putting his pencil to one side, had asked, 'However are we going to find places for all the people displaced by the cuts?' That did it. I didn't want to be found a job, with all the sinecurism that terrible observation implied. I was finally convinced that the RAF was no longer for me. Civil life, on the other hand, offered a secure base for the boys, who were at the final phase of entering productive life. David would shortly embark on solicitors' articles. Gregor, at the Regent Street Polytechnic, was a budding businessman. It was highly likely that if I stayed on in the RAF I would be posted overseas – probably to the Far East. All of these were arguments in favour of a premature retirement. The old life, moreover, had lost its appeal: a new one beckoned.

I had half seriously applied for the job of Secretary-General of the Association of British Travel Agents while I was at Colerne. The result had been shortlisting and an interview with the agency advising the Association. The interviewer was the son-in-law of Air Marshal Sir Clifford Sanderson. The interview went well but came to nothing. Now, after a week of particularly writhe-making frustration with Grandy, Burnett, Whitehall and all its works, I applied for the job of Under Treasurer of the Honourable Society of

163

Lincoln's Inn, one of the Inns of Court. Having, as always, done the homework of finding out all about it, I delivered the result to Mr Justice Buckley at the Royal Courts of Justice in the Strand. I thought I had a chance. But, as Hamlet found in the end, the rest was silence.

Not all was wasted. While we were living at Hendon David had spotted a job advertisement for the equivalent job of Under Treasurer of the Middle Temple. At once I began some research, including exploration of the beautiful gardens and buildings that the Middle shared with the Inner Temple (the Outer Temple long reduced to a vestige of offices off The Strand and part of the beaten track between the Courts and the two Inns).

The Temple was originally the property of the Knights Templar, the order of chivalry dissolved by the Pope and the King of France and virtually exiled to London. The transfer to lawyers by Edward III in 1338 and the agreement between the Middle and the Inner of 1732 might, I thought, come up in the interview, along with the start of the Wars of the Roses in the Middle Temple garden. As the Earl of Warwick says in Shakespeare's *Henry V*:

> *And here I prophesy: this brawl today*
> *Grown to this faction in the temple Garden*
> *Shall send between the Red Rose and the White*
> *A thousand souls to death and deadly night.*

With that and a look at the damage to the Temple Church, which unknowingly I had seen almost destroyed on the cataclysmic night of 11 May 1941 during my visit to London, I felt once again that I might be in with a chance.

I was. Soon after handing in my application to the Inn's offices in Middle Temple Lane, I was invited to a set of barristers' chambers in Pump Court, a blend of old buildings and harmonious new ones damaged in 1941 and overseen by an extremely able bencher, the late Eric Carpmael QC. I was welcomed by the head of chambers, Hubert Monroe QC, a leader at the tax bar; Sir Leslie Scarman, the first DASB and by then a High Court judge who later compiled a far-reaching study of London's inner city problems; and Martin

Jukes, who had left the bar to become Director General of the British Iron and Steel Federation, the steel industry's pressure group. We had an agreeable, almost bossy chat, at the end of which they told me to expect a further invitation to appear before a larger panel of other members of the Bench (government) of the Inn. As I left I saw the beautiful sundial on the ancient wall opposite inscribed with a mildly daunting observation:

> *Shadows we are and*
> *Like shadows depart.*

I felt it was trying to tell me something but I wasn't sure what.

I redoubled my researches, beating a path between the MOD and the Temple and slavering at the jaws at the prospect of what I saw as liberation. The summons soon came and I was ushered through the benchers' special entrance in Middle Temple Lane by a black-coated and stripe-trousered butler, Arthur Cubitt, later to become a friend and domestic mainstay. Assembled in one of the oak-panelled meeting rooms was a group of six of the thirty-odd benchers – judges and senior barristers selected by the old boy system that, I later decided, works very well. In the chair was another friend to be, the Treasurer of the Inn for the year 1968. He was the Honourable Ewen Montagu QC, Chairman (chief judge) of Middlesex Sessions, where he presided over criminal trials. He was also Judge Advocate to the Navy, providing legal guidance to courts marshal conducted by lay naval officers. He was a tall, striking figure, aquiline-featured and with a fearful temper, sometimes exploited by barristers for their own ends. But he was blessed with a marked sense of humour. The other benchers were a blur, as I always found during job interviews.

There were none of the penetrating questions I had expected from a bunch of professional examiners. But I did manage to convey my knowledge of the Inn and the law. They ended by inviting me to question them. In view, I asked half-seriously, of the orders made on 15 April 1630 by the Lord Keeper, the judges of both benches and the Barons of the Exchequer asserting that the Honourable Societies (of the Middle and Inner Temples) were instituted 'for the profession of the law and secondarily for the education of the sons of the nobility', what were the prospects for improving the training function of the Inn? The prospects were, they replied, what I chose to make them within the resources available – a disingenuous response, as I later found out, because the resources were non-existent. I had not stopped the show or raised the roof; but my question made an obvious impression.

They offered me the job at a salary of £2,500 a year, a large flat in the Temple with all costs paid and a free parking space within the often crammed central court. I applied at once for one of the premature releases from the services, known as Golden Bowlers, thrown up by the cuts in defence expenditure. They came with an enhanced gratuity and a pension not far short of the full amount due on my normal retirement date, which would have been twelve years later. Vice-Chief Brian Burnett asked me why I wanted to leave and I told him as much of the truth as my moral courage allowed, blaming primarily the idiotic RN-RAF clash. An air commodore from the personnel department sent for me and asked me to consider changing my mind: 'It's a good record, you know.' Euphoric at the prospect of becoming a civilian, I did not budge.

At once came shattering disillusionment. Ewen Montagu invited me to meet the office staff who worked in poky rooms below the panelled finery of the bench quarters. My doddering predecessor, in a roomful of mouldering memorabilia, told me of his forty-six years' service at the Inn. His next in line, the accountant, glared in hate because his application for the job had been turned down (he subsequently revealed himself as one of the most obnoxious people I had ever met). The students and renting officers had cubbyholes like a film set for *A Christmas Carol*. Montagu, semi-apologetic, explained that money would be spent on improvements to the building and the training I had asked about. I left in stupefied horror at what I had given up my career for, and went for a long walk along the Thames. I decided to call everything off, which would mean crawling back to the Vice-Chief and grovelling to Montagu at cancelling my acceptance. Just as I was about to knock on Montagu's door, Lord

Donovan, whom I would later regard as the best bencher, arrived and begged forgiveness for wanting to burst in ahead of me. He wanted, he said, to give the Inn the first copy of his government-commissioned report on the trade unions. I, of course, gave way. While they talked I decided to abide by my undertakings both to the RAF and to the Inn. The decision made me fear a return of the plague of depression. But it did not materialize, perhaps because I half sensed the possibility that the result might turn out as it has: the gateway to the far more useful and edifying life I have since enjoyed.

I slunk back to the office and wrote a minute to the Vice-Chief, with copies to Duke Mavor and the Assistant Under Secretary (Air) in case Burnett suppressed it. The post of DASB, I said, was justifiable only because of the gross over-manning of the air staff. The first need was to cut posts that existed only for taking in the washing of other posts. As to DASB, the rank should be reduced to group captain as a step towards abolition when the badly needed overhaul was complete. I thought of a verse of D.H. Lawrence's poem *Don'ts*:

> *Do hold yourself together and fight*
> *With a hit-hit here and a hit-hit there,*
> *And a comfortable feeling at night*
> *That you've let in a little air.*

Oh no I hadn't. There were a few reductions but they were soon restored. Meanwhile, for good or ill, I was out of the blue barathea and into the shiny serge of my only suit.

Chapter 22

Civil Suited

Thus what John Milton described as 'civil-suited morn' (*Il Pensoroso*) also suited me. As I settled down as Under Treasurer I ferreted out bits of the history of the Inner and Middle Temples. The deceased knights whose gravestones lay in the Temple Church were refugees from the Middle East in the Middle Ages. They brought their treasures with them and were given the site where the Inns now are. They needed a treasurer to keep their property safe and he needed an assistant. The need for their custodial services had long gone, but the titles have been kept for the very different duties they now performed. It was satisfying to know a little of the origins of the titles that Montagu and I had inherited.

Content to do the duties asked of me by my job amongst the lawyers, and well suited to be settled in the Temple with an ancient title, I remembered my attempt to dispense justice many years earlier in the Middle East. An airman, riled by having his decisions about his mealtimes made for him by a Flight Lieutenant Bates, had shouted, 'Fuck Bates, I'll make my own arrangements for breakfast,' and some idiot thereupon charged him with mutiny. That was when my interest in all things legal began. It was easy to discover from the *Manual of Air Force Law* (*MAFL*) kept by every RAF unit that the airman's outburst was no more than insubordination. There was no lesser alternative charge and he duly got off. Fast forwarding eight years to another quasi-legal encounter, I had to prosecute a corporal and a young airman for what would later be legalized as homo-sexual intercourse between consenting adults. Again the big blue manual came to my aid, enjoining me to do no more than present the facts dispassionately with no histrionics.

Otherwise, nothing remotely to do with law had come my way until boredom as a Vulcan squadron commander in 1958, coupled with the realization that I was still a London University student because of the exams in medicine I had taken, moved me to study for a law degree. An unexpected benefit from what I had learnt over the years was an antidote to the terrible feelings of confinement caused by the self-inflicted clipping of my RAF wings and entering the confines of the Temple. Learning the law had left me with a few bedraggled feathers of self-respect for the afterlife.

I took stock of what I knew. It was, of course, scarcely to be compared with the learning of a proper lawyer. It was more like the limited achievement of the patroness of one of the network of American dancing schools:

> *Arthur Murray*
> *Taught me dancing*
> *In a hurry.*

But at least I had fallen in love with the law and I knew what my new friends (not to mention a few anything but friends) in the Temple were on about. They kept it to themselves, often using tribal codes. *'Ex parte'*, for instance, means 'only partly'. *'In parte'* would have made more sense and it is as well that legal Latin has been made obsolete. A contrite bencher confessed to his colleagues that he had made a 'Derry and Peake' mistake, quoting a leading case (1889 LR 14 AC 337) and revealing only to the cognoscenti that he had knowingly made a reckless statement. (Even that was some-what cryptic, 'LR' being short for 'Law Reports' and 'AC' for 'Appeal Cases'.)

There were, I discovered, very few books for lay people about the wonderfully rich inheritance of guidance, in statute and statute laid down by judges that keeps lawyers on the rails. If I'd had the time, I would have written one.

Chapter 23

Reflections

Now in my 90th year I realize how lucky I am and how much there is to be thankful for. My wife Rachel – who passed away soon after her 90th birthday – and I have lived through astonishing changes. In 1938, as a boy in Malvern, I remember seeing a television set in an electrical equipment shop. It was mounted in a large lidded box with a mirror on the inside of the top to reflect and, I think, enlarge the blurred black and white image. The boxes got smaller, mirrors were no longer needed and the images became sharper and, many years later, coloured.

Similarly crude by present standards were telephones. Making a call depended on a live operator at one of a network of exchanges that extended all over the world. Ours was used a great deal by people in need of medical help from my father. Calls were either 'local' or 'trunk' (long distance). Some years later came 'STD' (Subscriber Trunk Dialling), enabling 'subscribers' to connect with astronomic numbers of telephones. I acknowledge that 'the blower' is hugely useful and convenient, but it remains a mixed blessing.

Changes in warfare have been no less astonishing. My father, like millions of others, served in the Army in the First World War and lived long enough to tell me of the use of what then were new or much improved weapons for killing people. As a doctor, he was categorized as a non-combatant, but commanding a field ambulance brought experience of soldiers who either died of their wounds or were maimed for life, despite his efforts and those of his comrades. He was gassed three times: the toxic effects caused him much suffering and eventually killed him.

One of the bereaved millions of the First World War was my mother, whose first husband and brother were killed on the Somme in the same week in 1916. 'Where have all the young men gone?' sang Marlene Dietrich in the 1960s. 'Known unto God' declares the gravestones of countless unknown soldiers. It saddens me to think that the so-called peace treaties made at the end of the First World War imposed conditions on Germany so extortionate as to practically pave the way for the Second World War.

The majority of my recollections are, of course, related to the 3,400-plus hours I spent aloft between 1940 and 1966 and the forty-seven types of aircraft I have flown – each a delight in its way. Civilian pilots nowadays build up far more hours, but they seldom fly more than Boeing or Airbus airliners.

By far the most delightful was every pilot's favourite – the Supermarine Spitfire designed by R.J. Mitchell before the Second World War, just in time for defending the country from onslaught by the Luftwaffe and one of two responses to an Air Ministry specification for a fighter armed with eight machine guns, four in each wing. The competitor was the Hawker Hurricane, which I never flew but it was enjoyed by other pilots for its performance only slightly less than that of the Spitfire. The genius of Mitchell's design wasn't fully apparent until the jet age, when it emerged that his aerofoil section (wing shape) would have been no less effective if it had been fitted to aircraft such as the supersonic Hunter.

I enjoyed the Spitfire as much as anybody, first encountering it as part of the type of flying that ended a refresher course at the Central Flying School (CFS). As I expected, it was a delight to fly, especially for aerobatics. A particularly difficult item was the eight-point or hesitation roll, involving a stop for a second or so as the roll progressed: it was all too easy to fall ignominiously out of the sky, which I often did. The only other aircraft in which I could do the same manoeuvre was the DH82 Tiger Moth, whose light wing-loading made it easy.

My love affair with the Spitfire revived while I was back at the CFS as an examiner. It was requited unexpectedly when an ex-commandant promoted to Air Marshal and Commander-in-Chief of RAF stations in Germany needed to secure a future for the purloined Spitfire – reconnaissance version, unarmed, light blue and adorned with his initials – that he used as a personal conveyance for visits. At the end of his tour as commander-in-chief he needed to find a home for it. Having been commandant of CFS some years beforehand and conscious of its collegiate tradition, he gave it to his old school. Happily, there were only two pilots at the school qualified to fly Spitfires. One was the commandant, much too busy and disinclined to bother. The other was me. Knowing that to keep an aircraft serviceable it must be flown from time to time, I duly flew it once a week or so. Being a lifelong show-off, I ended these flights with a short display of aerobatics over the airfield as an entertainment for the people below, which included hesitation rolls. Whether the low pass at the ground would end with the aircraft the right way up or upside down, which posture could be maintained for the thirteen seconds that the fuel flow would last, was decided by our two children, then aged four and six, who took it in turns to choose between the two.

I had love affairs with other aircraft. Next on the list was the Avro Vulcan. Named after one of the Roman pantheon of gods, its basic design dated back to 1947. A prototype first flew in 1951, leading to an order for eighty-nine aircraft in 1955. The last aircraft was sold for breaking up in 1993. The other two in this trio were the Vickers Valiant, relatively slow and cumbersome and memorable only because it was used to drop the British atomic bomb on Christmas Island, and the Victor – the subject of banter because of what looked like the precarious attachment of its tail.

The Vulcan was a bomber that thought it was a fighter. Its enormous wing area gave it manoeuverability akin to that of much smaller aircraft. So much so that when it was used for what was called 'fighter affiliation', the Vulcan could swap roles with its adversary. I found it a refreshing change from flying straight and level as the target for quarter attacks (curving approaches to the back end), when the fighter did the straight and level bit and the Vulcan did the attacking. The other enjoyable change from endless practice bombing were the displays that we were often required to give at Battle of Britain days and similar events in different parts of the world; usually a beat-up – a dive almost to ground level – followed by a steep climb at full power.

I also liked the Airspeed Oxford, on which I had trained, admirably difficult to land because of its habit of veering off the straight and narrow. Similarly challenging for the same reason was the Harvard, in which I taught advanced flying at Cranwell and learned a great deal myself, especially how to perform aerobatics. Another swinger was the Hastings, immensely enjoyable because of the faraway places its long range enabled me to visit.

Lacking the challenge of difficulty of handling was the Dakota, beast of burden and dropper of parachutists and their needs. It remains a very versatile and adaptable aircraft, one version having been fitted with floats. Its greatest claim to fame was supporting the Allies during the Second World War when it was a vital element in the liberation of France, the epic operation over Arnhem and the Rhine crossing shortly before the Armistice. Dating back to the early 1930s and developed from the DC2, it remains in use in many parts of the world and is something of a marvel.

During my first tour of bomber operations I was glad that our base at Fayid in the Canal Zone had a pre-war leftover – a Fairey Gordon. The other pilots and I treated it as a fun aircraft, but in its day it would have been a bomber. It was easier to fly than its predecessors, being fitted with wing flaps that facilitated slower final approaches. Fayid also housed a Lysander high-wing monoplane. In the European Theatre it was used to drop, and occasionally to land, undercover agents working in German-occupied France, as well as lifting those who had finished their tours or had to escape.

I was no less attracted to what were known as 'puddle jumpers'. My first encounter was at Odiham, where there was an Auster, misused as a runabout. Its real use was reconnaissance for the ground troops later organized as the Army Air Corps.

The jet age offered many attractions. My first encounter was with the Meteor – a delight to fly and excellent for aerobatics. Even more enjoyable was the Vampire, wonderfully manoeuvrable. I flew it in the Far East to provide the trainee controllers of the Singapore Auxiliary Air Force with a fighter to vector towards a target Valetta. I went on to fly the biggest and smallest jets of all – respectively, the Vulcan and the Hunter. Both of them were thoroughly enjoyable. Indeed, I can't remember any aircraft that weren't. Only the Lancaster, mainstay of Bomber Command during the Second World War, had controls that needed unusual strength to exercise.

Brightest and best, perhaps, were the special challenges posed by gliders. Flying them meant that, once launched, there were none of the get-out-of-trouble options of powered flight, such as going round again after a dodgy approach or a bungled landing. On the other hand, the use of upward currents of air, known as thermals, could be used to gain height and travel great distances. That I never had a chance to experience, having been asked to teach the elements of being launched and returning safely to terra firma at Cranwell to officers' wives, and later, at Colerne, to members of the resuscitated Bannerdown Gliding Club in the T21 trainer. I never went solo in the club's Grunau Baby, a sports model of which the moving spirit of the club had used to good effect. My association with gliders came later with the Horsa and Hamilcars of the Glider Pilot Regiment, which carried infantry and their equipment to the dropping zones on D-Day, at Arnhem, and across the Rhine. Inevitably, some of them crash-landed. One unfortunate platoon commander, asked to report his position, replied that he was 'up to the arse in plywood'.

I worried, like other air-struck young men, about whether I would make the grade. But the moment David Bamford let me handle a Tiger Moth, my worry evaporated. I took to the Tiger Moth like a fish to water. The same was true across the whole range of aircraft, gliders included, that it fell to me to fly during the next twenty-six years. When I taught flying I discovered that a small minority of fortunate would-be pilots have the same experience: all the instructor needs to do is to show them how not to kill themselves and let them get on with it.

Old airmen, including me, are prone to boasting about the length of their service. I was thankful to shed my airman's number, derisively compared to the population of China, and acquire an officer's taunt-proof equivalent. Merciless banter didn't stop there: in my day as an AC (aircraftsman, second class) I had to perform the rite of passage of being sent to the stores to draw a non-existent skyhook. I only hope such mickey-taking has lasted down the arches of the years.

Long gone, I hope, is the snobbery about length of service behind the taunt 'Get some in' and its tropical version, 'Get your knees brown.' At one time there was a prejudice against crews who flew run-of-the-mill missions in what were regarded as humdrum aircraft. The Britannia transports at Lyneham, for instance, were known as 'shiny ships', and compared favourably with the humble Hastings. Even grander were the crews of the Comet, who started their trips later and finished them earlier than their less fortunate colleagues. Sadly, one of the much-admired Comets crashed into the Mediterranean. After one of the most exhaustive investigations ever conducted, the conclusion was that a design fault made it unsafe. Much modified, it became the Nimrod. That too proved to be anything but the mighty hunter that its name connotes: a defective fuel system caused a fatal crash in Afghanistan. A House of Commons debate led to its withdrawal from service and a protest about the resulting waste.

In maudlin moments, I have reflected that mankind never refrains from using new discoveries for war. As far back as the age of bows and arrows, when the English longbow out-shot its French competitor, the urge has been to develop more and more lethal weaponry, and correspondingly, defensive protection. The Lee-Enfield rifle has been superseded by the Kalashnikov. Machine guns such as the Browning, with huge rates of fire, have made single-shot guns semi-obsolete. Far and away the worst weaponry, of course, has emerged with the arrival of the nuclear, later thermonuclear, age. The weapons are uniquely evil because their effects cannot be limited; they can slaughter millions of living creatures, cause genetic damage, and contaminate the earth for many thousands of years. Man's inhumanity to man has given place to man's suicidal inhumanity to the planet, and the bravado that accompanies his Gadarene determination to destroy it. My shame at having been part of it as a Vulcan pilot is mitigated only by decades of membership of the Campaign for Nuclear Disarmament (CND).

Even so, delight in aircraft has permeated much of my life. From my encounter as a teenager with Sir Alan Cobham's flying circus to my final touch-down in my forties, across the gamut of types from the Tiger to the Hastings via forty-odd others, I have derived enormous satisfaction, fulfilment and often ecstasy.

As American Second World War aviator John Gillespie Magee (1922–41) put it in his famous poem *High Flight*:

> *Oh I have slipped the surly bonds of earth*
> *And danced the skies on laughter-silvered wings*
> *Sunward I've climbed and joined the tumbling mirth*
> *Of sun-split clouds – and done a hundred things*
> *You have not dreamed of;*
> *wheeled and soared and swung*
> *High in the sun-lit silence. Hovering there*
> *I've chased the wind along through footless halls of air*
> *Up, up, the long delirious burning blue*
> *I've topped the wind-swept heights with easy grace*
> *And while with silent lifting mind I've trod*
> *The high, untrespassed sanctity of space*
> *Put out my hand and touched the face of God.*

So have I.

Index